what can a woman do with a camera?

edited by jo spence and joan solomon

what can a woman do with a camera?

photography for women

SCARLET PRESS

Published by Scarlet Press
5 Montague Rd, London E8 2HN

British Library Cataloguing-in-Publication Data
A catalogue record for this book is available from the
British Library.

ISBN 185727 077 0 pb
      185727 082 7 hb

The publishers wish to thank Birmingham Museums and
Art Gallery for permission to use *Pretty Baa Lambs* by
Ford Maddox Brown in Claire Collison's work.

Designed by Suzanne Perkins/Grafica
Printed in Hong Kong

contents

to Jo Spence

Jo was my aunt, but I saw her as a big sister and a friend. She was many things: capable, confident, outspoken, passionate and angry, with a sense of fun, humour and adventure. She died in June 1992.

She affected my life in many ways, one of the most significant being in the use of my camera. It was in the last few years of her life that I started to challenge my own ideas about photography. This still goes on today as, like Jo did for years, I keep a photographic diary.

Her phototherapy has influenced many people. 'Ordinary' people have picked up their cameras and recorded their lives, questioning the world in an attempt to understand their truths. Her courageous step to turn her back on conventional medicine when she developed cancer has also been influential. She chose to radically change her diet and, among other treatments, to use herbal remedies. I am certain this path helped her last year to be a bit more tolerable and a little less painful. This has made me re-evaluate my own diet and lifestyle.

Jo was a workaholic, always enthusiastic and wanting to hear people's stories, which often led to more photographic work. She was selfless. When she discovered she had breast cancer she didn't tell us (my dad, sister or myself) for fear of worrying and hurting us. It was only when she was diagnosed as having leukaemia that she admitted she was ill, probably terminally. We became very close as we discovered we had interests and traits in common, but she still didn't tell me of her physical and spiritual pain.

I want to say thank you to Jo for opening my eyes to a different perspective on my conventional life.

Lisa Clode

preface

The initial research and exploration into the significance of the family album was begun by Jo Spence in 1975 and continued until her death in June 1992. Building on this work, Jo Spence and Nina Kellgren interviewed women as family historians and archivists. The idea of a book was further developed in conjunction with Bushy Kelly and Sue Isherwood, who together with Jo Spence and Joan Solomon initiated solo projects. The final structuring, editorial writing and weaving together was done by Joan Solomon. That is the genesis of our book.

When two people work together as closely as Jo and I have done in producing this book (and far beyond that), an alchemy transforms what each person brings to it into something greater than the two contributions added together. Where and how that chemistry took place is hard to say – I think from a place of fun and loving which was always alight as we worked. The unbearably fragile crucible that lay between us, holding and fashioning our offerings, has disappeared into silence. With my own base metal, I hope I have been able to do justice to Jo in finishing our book in a way that she would have wanted. May it be a tribute to the wonderful woman who has most profoundly touched the hearts and minds of many.

My thanks go to all the contributors to this book for their warm co-operation, to friends who gave me their time and advice, to Avis Lewallen and Caroline North, who acted as able and sensitive midwives, to John Camino-Jones for his unfailing faith in our project and to Louis Solomon for his loving support.

Joan Solomon
Bristol
March 1995

joan solomon

introduction

There is a version of femininity which tells us that women are passive, gentle, dependent, emotional, somewhat illogical, home-makers and madonna/mothers. It is an old myth kept firmly entrenched and constantly repeated, constructed over and over again through representations of women. Many of us have at some time or another bought into this 'doll's house' image of supposed femininity, as well as the idea that we are seductive, alluring and sexy. Women's actual experience tells a different story. There is a split between the fictitious woman represented publicly and how we know our daily and our private selves to be. How can we as women tell stories that eradicate the disparity between how we are seen and what we feel? How do we present who we really are in terms of images? And why does it matter that we do?

To answer this we need to understand the very fundamental way that the representation of people helps to determine who they become. In a world where an oral tradition has been almost lost, where agendas and stories have been constructed through the institution of the 'mass media', how do we know who we are? From the moment we are born, while we are growing up and in fact throughout our lives, we contact daily a welter of representations of what we *may* become. It is through this very contact with the myriad possibilities conveyed in images, plus the ways in which we are positioned in society in terms of our gender, class, race and sexual orientation, that we become who we are. When we encounter images of what and how women are supposed to be, we need to know that the 'supposed' is a construct, a product of representations. We know already that we are not like the stereotypes presented to us, yet we have all seen young women still trying to be like the images, made mostly by men, fed through magazines. We need, with our own images, to redefine ourselves as we know ourselves to be, but before we can hope to get anywhere with images, we need to disclose ourselves to ourselves.

Even this raises questions. What 'self' are we disclosing? It is through our connections with our family, society and culture we experience ourselves in the world. The self only comes into being in relationship and through the constant encounters with representations around us. In taking up our positions in the family and in society our multi-layered self is always shifting. Identity is never static, nor unified in one essential self. How, then, can we make our subjective selves visible; how do we give them material form? Not only how, but can it be done at all? What we can do with the images we make is to vigorously interrogate desire, fear, shame, anger, sexuality, motherhood, class, love and so on. In other words, we can deconstruct. We can explore all our societal and relational connections in an attempt to break down the fiction presented as woman.

Painful encounters with the self can stimulate a process whereby we are enabled to create new ways of seeing and representing ourselves. Exploring intimate networks of relationships is never easy, as they lie at the heart of our deepest feelings, often unresolved, and often involve difficult loyalties. Nor is it easy to creep behind the idealisations which come into being to mask early childhood pain. It is a matter of moving through thickets of screen memories, fantasies and dreams to make our own images, ones which do represent our lives as we experience them. Our aim is to take the reader on a visual and verbal journey, to show that in using our cameras as a form of visual diary, in disclosing ourselves to ourselves, we can empower ourselves and each other.

There is little in amateur or popular photography magazines to help us map our course. There, the concept of photography is limited, being addressed mainly to white heterosexual males. Not much is offered to women and the existence of working-class, black or lesbian experience is barely acknowledged. It is orientated primarily to 'know-how' and assumes an interest in tourism, the landscape and glamour. In this genre attitudes to women are unhelpful. Take, for instance, articles which demonstrate how to light and photograph the 'nude'. Articles such as this appear in almost every photographic magazine and are often accompanied by images which border on soft porn. In reality they're thinly veiled invitations to gaze at women's bodies. Women are used decoratively, often to advertise photographic products. When they are shown as users of equipment, the images are of slender hands with immaculately manicured nails delicately holding a very simple camera, the implication being that even a woman can manage this.

But there is another practice that we encounter through popular photography: the whole complex business of 'snapshotting'. Here the conventions are intimately linked to accessible technology:

easy-to-use cameras, film which is widely available and mostly affordable, and fast-delivering processing depots which are popping up in every high street and shopping mall, ideal for recording all family matters. Here women are recognised as users, as keepers of the family album. It is not difficult to persuade people to take snapshots of pleasurable moments. In amateur photography journals and camera clubs, competitions for the best landscape, best baby, best holiday, best bride are rife. From this standpoint readers or members are invited to move through countless stereotypes of babies and family groups within a wider stereotyping of class, race and gender. Such journals and clubs emphasise how to get 'better results', insidiously encouraging us to spend money on equipment and gadgets while repeatedly stating how easy the whole thing is. Eastman, the largest of all photographic companies, grew on their slogan 'You push the button, we do the rest.' Indeed, the simplest camera will do, but 'snapshotting' is not just a matter of picking up a camera, pointing it and pressing the shutter.

In taking the simplest photograph we are choosing what to photograph and, just as importantly, we are deciding what to leave out. How often do we snap the messy rooms around our teenage children, or our babies amidst their clutter? Yet these contexts would give clues which would change the readings of our photographs. Sometimes we leave out what we think is too private or painful to share, or what would put our families in a bad light. So we follow conventional ways of presenting our families, ways learned from photographic magazines, on holidays, at weddings, on birthdays and other celebrations; ways which satisfy our longing for how we would like our families to be, loving and magically 'happy ever after'. Though no family is like this, there are enough fragments of fun caught by our cameras to present ourselves to ourselves in an idealised way. Thus family values are re-inscribed along very traditional lines. Women adopt these agendas and usually use cameras only to record events and capture surfaces.

Our starting point will also be the domestic private world, the minutiae of daily living; a world most women easily inhabit. Women are most often the archivists or historians in maintaining the 'family album', in diary writing, in the keeping of scrapbooks and personal memorabilia. We look at all these and we use the term 'family album' to mean that collection of life moments where what is positive in family experience has been recorded, while disruptions, dangerous connections and difficult changes have been omitted and rendered invisible. Snapshots are part of and create family folklore and mythologies. We will address this once unproblematic document, the 'family album', with all its omissions, and, given that traditional family structures are rapidly changing, we will refer to 'households' as well as families. The idea is to keep and question documents about the self, to make life maps, to tell visual stories and gradually to develop an historical imagination; to move memory beyond the nostalgic.

In creating this book the late Jo Spence and I have been particularly concerned to have women use their cameras in ways which go beyond the usual photographic preoccupations with surface and lighting, the concern of much of the literature of amateur photography; past the 'smiling public faces' of the family festivals that go to make up the family album; beyond the advertiser's art, which conceals the immense diversity of women and represents us as homogenised Barbie dolls; to embark on an inner journey. To this end, the book is blatantly personal, attempting to help create a sense of safety in which the reader can consider her own life and the possibility of using her camera differently. The idea is to make visible our everyday life: surroundings, work, politics, interests and institutional contexts. The point is to remove ourselves from the usual 'happy snaps' of the idealised family and engage with the discomforts and conflicts and even crises lying beneath the surfaces of family outings and weddings: in other words, to engage with the psychic reality of our lives. This would of necessity have to go against the stream of never-ending images coming at us from every level of our lives, telling us how we should look, how we should be and who we are.

This book is divided into five sections though inevitably the boundaries are blurred. In structuring it we have visualised a movement outward from our own private centre to a context within the family and then to a wider political context. To begin with we address the question of recording our lives. Jo Stanley's 'Accounting for our days' explains why diaries matter, giving an overview of the significance of diary writing. Women have chosen various ways to document their lives. Some have opted for straightforward 'naturalistic' snapshotting. However, as Maggie Murray reminds us in questioning documentary photography, there are always unseen and unknown complexities behind the most naturalistic-looking photograph, even if they lie only in why the photographer has selected just that moment to depict. Text amplifies the meanings of the pictures. Joyce Leketi-Solomon documents great battles with her weight and with her studies and gives us a glimpse into an 'unofficial' family history with pictures of her student peer group. Here we have a hint of the way young girls use photographs to assert their individuality and independence, levels of experience which do not find their way into the family album. Jean Wythe also uses text with naturalistic images, taking the reader beyond their surface meaning into surprising places. Occasionally, in recording aspects of their lives, women have 'staged' scenes transforming feelings into images, which are then sometimes even further manipulated. Janet Edmeades has worked in this way, conveying very powerfully what having asthma feels like, while Claire Collison, who has also chosen this technique, explores spiritual/physical strength, women/nature and illness.

From personal accounts of women's lives we move on to family matters, though separating women's recording of their lives from 'the family' is arbitrary, as we are all bedded in the family, either that of our origin or the one we have created. My own work uses mostly constructed images to recreate a sense of invisibility and childhood pain and deals with the difficulties of not belonging at any level, while Brenda Prince's beautiful, simple letter to her mother, exposing the complex feelings of parents and daughter in coming to terms with her lesbianism, shows her overcoming the difficulty of being outside the narrow confines of social acceptance. This is the stuff of family politics, as is the work of Elizabeth-Anne Williams, whose snapshots of chickens and washing lines, together with their text, draw us to the realisation that she is talking about the struggles of trying to develop herself as a person from the position of being a wife and mother. In a very different idiom, in which text and image work together, Clarissa Sligh bears witness to the ways in which she and her family have been wounded. Rosy Martin, using constructed images and simple snapshots, reveals one of the most intimate moments of a family's history, not normally included in the family album: the death of a parent. In a piece also emanating indirectly from her father's death, Lisa Chell deals with transience. Here, naturalistic pictures work purely symbolically.

Going far beyond the microcosm of family politics, we turn to wider political contexts. Nilofar Akmut shows the personal as political and historic in the tearing apart of a family through the implications of the partitioning of India. The work ranges widely. Sylvia Ayling takes in a sweep of women's history using her camera as an antidote to media bias. Alice Dennett makes direct political comments from the standpoint of a working-class pensioner documenting her class position from the inside, while Maggie Murray examines the politics of being a documentary photographer, her camera pointed at 'other people'. Linda Troeller's examination of society's treatment of terminally ill patients sensitively negotiates the ethical and moral dilemmas facing photographers looking at other people's lives: her work arose out of a need to connect painful personal memories to the plight of those suffering from AIDS. It starts from a poignant re-examination of her mother's stigmatisation in having TB and makes the connection with what it is like living with AIDS.

With enormous courage, staring with unusual honesty into the darkest places of the soul, Jo Spence demonstrates the process of gaining access to buried memories and suppressed feelings, revealing how the richness of women's stories can be mined. She shows how an unravelling of the past helps her to understand the present. Her method of restaging the past, revealing how empowering the disclosure of secrets can be, has developed into a technique of phototherapy. No less important are the unearthing of the large political secrets which shape our lives.

What we have in this collection is a collage of women's everyday lives, histories and fantasies which are unique, personal and varied. Here is an invitation to women to look very differently at their lives and, most importantly, never to denigrate what we have or do. What may seem narcissistic and self-indulgent on one level must be seen as only part of a process which has its importance in locating women's personal history in a wider political context. It is important for women to move to a wide arena, that which includes work, social endeavour and politics in their broadest sense, with the connections and obligations that they entail; areas which are in a way marginalised through this society's obsessive emphasis on the 'the family'. In the fourth section we have shown how women have, on a practical level, taken photography out into the public domain; how women sharing personal histories have ended up making political statements. This is how Beryl Graham worked with Rosy Thornton and the Welbeck Road Mothers and Toddlers Group to produce 'Mothers of invention'.

Groups working on political issues have turned their personal predicaments into exhibitions. Claire Grey worked with a group of unemployed, homeless young people in a hostel and during the process of 'breaking through their lethargy, a disabling feature of homelessness', was born the idea for a public exhibition which they called 'Down But Not Out'. Work with photographs can begin really early, as is shown in the wonderful work, already politicised, with primary school children done by Kamina Walton.

What begins as personal history becomes, when replicated again and again, the 'buzz and implication' of history. We invite new insights into the power of photography, showing how we can, with our cameras, provide the opportunity to move away from being looked at as passive objects and position ourselves as makers of our own images.

Finally, we offer advice in practicalities. In her article 'Taking the pictures', Anne Hickmott leads us through choices around cameras and film and talks about how to make our images, and the editors suggest practical ways of getting started.

Our hope is that this book will be used to stimulate ideas and discussion which will challenge received ideas about ourselves and that it will encourage women to use their cameras fearlessly as tools of exploration.

recording our lives

jo stanley

accounting for our days

3 July 1992, Upper Holloway

The day after Jo's funeral. I'm still wearing the same clothes, though she feels very gone. End of continuity. This morning in bed started to write about the funeral in my Death novella, but it came out as a straight, factual diary account anyway, so I stuck it into my diary. This afternoon talked to Routledge about editing *Cultural Sniping*. [1] Getting out of lift there was stunned by vision of lobby like an umbrella park. I miss not having Jo's camera, or any decent one to take a picture. Went to Silver Moon to get books on black women's diaries for chapter in Jo's book with Joan. Found none specifically, but got some good stuff anyway that will also feed into October's WEA class on women's history. How the hell do I survive financially? Felt good that Silver Moon is expanding. All this huge space for us!

This is my (rather self-conscious) diary for that day. I've included it because it says a number of things significant to this chapter on the history of women's diary writing. These things include:

Companionship
For me as for many women, my diary is a friend to moan to, explore with, celebrate in, use for listing and accounting to myself, and a place in which to continually plan the past and future versions of my life.

Fiction/fact
The relationship between diary writing and fiction is a close one. I could have validly written about the funeral in either form. Feeling free to write it as fiction paradoxically freed me to write it as non-fiction – often it works the other way round.

Absences of marginalised groups
I had to very energetically, for this essay, seek black women's history. It's not lying round, or on GCSE syllabi like the life accounts of white Europeans Virginia Woolf or Anne Frank. It's not even published.

Freedom to be multi-faceted
Diaries are a place for subjectively writing about or portraying both personal feelings and external events of significance, e.g., that a feminist bookshop in a western capital in the early 1990s has grown into large new premises.

Lifestyle
It shows that the writer, me, like a woman shooting her own life records, has got the time, confidence, literacy and self-interest to write about her life, unlike millions of our foremothers.

Consciousness of audience
Knowing it will probably be published affects the freedom with which I write. For example, I wasn't up-front about the misery I felt at some hostility in Silver Moon. I censored a reference to my silver sneakers, and I hesitated over whether to write 'Spence' after the name 'Jo'. In painting it would be termed an 'exhibition piece'.

Addressing you
It's a kind of letter to you, my reader, like a snap taken for a friend to see. It is also a record of unaudienced activity I did for my own ends.

A kind of snap
It functions in the stead of a camera. I note photographs I might have taken – of the umbrellas, for instance – and I try to write with the fast vividness of a camera.

This chapter looks at how we learn about our own and other women's journeys in life through our journals, through the aegis of this companion with which we may never have expected to go public. I will use the words diaries and journals interchangeably, defining both as 'a book of days'.

Why is there a chapter on words in a book on pictures?
This section on diaries is included in a book on women and photography to show how, by recognising the parallels between a written self-history and a photographic one, we can think about the ideas, opportunities and constraints that affect the ways women record their lives. Firstly, pictures, like written records, are another way of looking at/for women's history. Secondly, writing and painting tools have been about for 4,000 years, but camera technology hasn't always been available – and still isn't for

impoverished people in Britain and in less developed countries. Photography, therefore, provides a new and dramatic way of recording, communicating and understanding aspects of women's lives. Thirdly, journals are a useful complement and contrast to photos. Because of the depths of feeling they can encompass, they can show 20th-century women researchers direct visual evidence that might have been written out of official histories. This might include lesbian women's experiences, like Edith Simcox's love of the writer George Eliot, [2] or 19th-century Afro-American women's literacy, leadership skills and professional work. Fourthly, journals – be they pictorial or written – are usually women's *own* accounts, where we are not posed or snapped by another to the usual extent. Slave journals, narrated to white campaigners, are an obvious contrast to this. We are usually subject, not object, in journals, which are more like the private pictures we take alone with remote control or in photo booths, unaccompanied by a photographer and choosing the seat height, the curtains, the background colour and so on for ourselves. A photographic or written record can offer us the room to be more profoundly real, more wildly posey, more lusciously creative, more outrageously critical, more *anything* than any other medium. And we can do that entirely for our own eyes, if we want.

Why do diaries matter?
Why do other women's diaries matter to us now? Simply because, published or unpublished, they tell us versions of other women's lives. It's really only in the last two decades that women's history, particularly that of marginalised women, has begun to be properly researched, and, of course, we're finding that it's too late. Too many people have died.

Women's lives are barely known because the class and sex and cultural group that has recorded history is the group that has also deemed women's, especially black women's, lives not worthy of attention. Women's history is evidenced, though, to some extent, in accounts we have recorded ourselves, primarily for ourselves: diaries, letters, jottings. In the same way, photography can be used to make a visual record of contemporary women's lives, and this time we can be central, and not on the sidelines. In diaries, we can give – conscious of a future audience or not – a version of who we are, what we've been doing, what we care about. We can even indicate aspects of our mothers', grandmothers', friends' and sisters' lives.

But who writes diaries and how?
Looking at the manuscript diaries in the Fawcett Library's archives, I was suddenly struck by a realisation about the gender and class implication in the term 'diary'. I had unproblematically held the

idea that 'diary' meant a book. Actually this assumes privilege: that the creator of the diary had the time and self-respect to put her records into neat book form. In fact, a lot of diaries are incomplete. Letters, menus, cuttings and pressed flowers are sometimes loosely contained between the blank pages – presumably on the assumption that one day there would be time to stick those bits in and write that page up. And some diaries are not bound at all, but just kept in archive boxes, as our own self-records today might be shoved in carrier bags or old box files. This whole practice suggests that bound and neatly completed diaries may be rare. Certainly they are more likely to have been kept by leisured men rather than working-class women.

As for writing, and the right to write, the knowledge women had or needed may have included arithmetic, star systems, seasons and chemical properties, but many learned this orally, from other busy women. However, those who were most beleaguered and most wise may well have tried to learn to write records because of a sense of historical importance. 'In medieval Europe and England... diaries were kept by "witches" attempting to preserve pagan wisdom. If a witch's diary were discovered, not only would the book be burned, its writer might be burned as well.' [3] In 1818, over 80 per cent of children in England and Wales still had no access to education and would grow up illiterate. It was 19th-century British industrialisation and the moral fears of Christians that brought in a – limited – education system. By 1900, only 5 per cent of surveyed women and men were defined 'illiterate'.

The kinds of diaries that exist

I propose that there are three main groupings for the historical diaries we read: impersonal, personal and collective, though some may overlap. I've developed this idea from looking at published diaries (and therefore largely those of well-connected Europeans). Those which have not been published may fall into similar categories but that can never really be comprehensively proved.

Impersonal diaries

Just as some women photographers today document themselves at key moments, at a Pride march, for example, so some journals are created by witnesses of important moments in history. Take, for instance, Afro-American anti-slavery campaigner Sojourner Truth's story, which she narrated to a friend and which was then published, or Agnes Smedley's early 20th-century articles from China. These tend to be women's descriptions of external events such as war and major social change, not primarily an exploration of their reaction to those events. They usually read as if they are written with the expectation of an audience one day.

Millicent Garrett Fawcett (1847–1929) kept two sorts of records of her 1901 visit to English concentration camps in South Africa – or at least that's the form in which they survive in the Fawcett Library. One great cathedral of a book, in crimson gold-tooled leather, is the picture account. It has photographs of the camps and even of her sewing on the ship. Each stiff, cream page of small black and white glossy photographs is stitched between a printed page of the official government report on the camps (which she helped to write). The most personal elements are those from other people – a poem someone copied out by hand for her, for example. [4]

The other record of her visit to the camps is a four-inch thick wadge of cream quarto paper – handwritten notes rather than a diary. It's been written fast; the lines almost jostle each other and the whole collection is gathered in one perforated corner by some embroidered silk, to which an eau-de-nil pencil stump is attached. Read together, pictures and handwriting tell a complex but still fairly impersonal story.

In only one case have I been able to find a woman's own account of a political event mixed in the same volume as the newspaper images and words about it. Miss Marjory Lees (whose mum had been mayor of Oldham) was the president of Oldham Women's Suffrage Society in Lancashire. She kept a record of the big suffragist pilgrimage to London which she joined in July 1913. The first 20 pages are of newspaper cuttings about the route, the women on the march, their final reception and speeches. The second half consists of 20 very closely written pages of personal account of the pilgrimage. It is written rather dutifully, as if for the society's members; more of a letter than a personal account. [5]

Other diaries are written with a campaigning polemical function, for example White South African Ruth First's book *117 Days*. [6] It excited public reaction to private experience – in this case, of solitary confinement for fighting apartheid.

Some diaries are written solely for historical purposes at another's behest. Mass Observation is an example of this in post-1930s Britain. The archives in the University of Sussex are an important insight into the reactions of the self-selected social observers of a period – predominantly white, middle-aged, middle-class, single women. Some diarists regurgitate, unchallenged, the received wisdom of the period, so that to read them is almost like reading the monolithic jingoism of a popular newspaper's 'diarist'.

Personal diaries
Journals can be written privately but later, often posthumously, made public. Anne Frank's account [7] of her secret attic life in occupied Holland is the best-known European example of this. Japanese court women in the 10th and 11th centuries, such as Lady Sarashina and Sei Shonagon [8] 'developed the diary into a form of

personal expression that explored subjective fantasies and fiction, not just external realities'. [9]

The most private diaries are secret, locked, and written for personal exploration, solace, and philosophical reflection. Known examples of these include those of 19th-century Quakers, people searching for transcendence such as Thoreau, or those carrying out intensive self-exploration, like psychologist Carl Jung.

Literary journals are written by a writer as a notebook, a site of unstructured exploration, record of work, warm-up place. This is one of the uses to which writer Virginia Woolf put her journals in the early decades of this century. And some of the most important diaries are 'fiction'. An example of this is the novel *The Golden Notebook*. [10] Here, Doris Lessing's character, Anna Wulf, has four diaries (black, red, yellow, blue) which she uses before finding she can manage some kind of synthesis: a fifth journal, the golden one.

Collective journals
Collective journals really belong to the 'impersonal' category. A patchwork quilted by a group of women could be a functional and three-dimensional form of accounting for lives on an American frontier. But other forms of group journal might be those written by a creative writing class or a women's artists' group, like that in 1980s Brixton. [11] Each member takes her weekly turn, then the accumulated sheets are turned into a whole account of a group's year.

Jo Spence would have liked me to write at length about collective journals. She had the idea that some groups of women somewhere might have created shared political albums, as middle-class women created Victorian scrap albums. Jo's former partner, Terry Dennett, found, looking at male-organised groupings like the 19th-century Clarion clubs, that such albums 'grew spontaneously out of the popular scrapbook form, typically a collection of notes, press cuttings, quotations and political ephemera which every radical collected for her or his own use… as a repository and an archive of the life and activities of the group… [including] signatories of famous Labour personalities… minutes of meetings, political speeches… election leaflets'. [12]

There may actually be albums, for instance, from co-op women's or Labour party branches, but I couldn't locate any. With some proud exceptions, British women in the last 200 years or so, especially mothers, seem to have largely worked in isolation from other women. Therefore the most collective diary/album would really be the family album – with all its perpetuated rules and lies.

However, in the area of the Fawcett Library's archives nicknamed 'The Treasures' there are documents which almost approach the collective diary idea. Looking at relics of suffrage groups, women's emigration societies and women's trade unions, two main forms of records are visible. A group's daily happenings as seen by one member can be learned through the minute books of meetings. These are usually written in formal style with little personal detail. The telling information is in the misplaced items lodged in the minute books' pages: an airmail letter saying 'Thank you for asking about my children,' or 'Did you get over your rheumatic cold?' Examples of minutes-style diaries include those of the British Women's Emigration Society (1885–1919) and the Catholic Women's Suffrage Society/St Joan's Social and Political Alliance (1911–54). [13]

Secondly, the group's daily doings – as seen by the media – are recorded in newspaper cuttings albums, often kept by the newspaper committee or the cuttings secretary. These are not annotated. No album I have seen contains a spontaneous response to any articles scribbled on the stiff pages next to the articles. There's no graffiti like 'Load of bunk. Stupid reporter!' And, of course, no fluorescent highlighting. In every example I've seen, there is no amalgamation of the personal and the political. No snaps are included in the cuttings album or minute book. Nor does the minute book ever stray into the cuttings book territory. It's a very ordered world. There's a sense that these women assumed they were not permitted to insert their private selves into these political histories. I think that's about an attitude of the period: that the personal was private. But maybe because they were such thoroughly politicised characters, they might not have felt that a dichotomy or absence existed.

Perhaps the nearest example of a mixture of the personal and political diary of a group is almost accidental, and transgresses the normal diary boundaries. In Australian suffrage campaigner Vida Goldstein's records of the first International Women's Suffrage Conference, in Washington DC, 1902, there's an autograph album. [14] In it, people have written not only their signatures, but affectionate messages and poems and in some cases have stuck in photos of their (grand) homes or cartes de visite. It's the most personal record of a major public event I've yet come across – and is sort of collective. However, it was always in Vida Goldstein's personal possession until it was donated to a women's library after her death in the 1950s.

Who sees them? Who censors them?
We have seen from the discussion about personal and impersonal diaries that the distinction is a usefully clarifying one, but that the picture is not one of discrete categories. Not only did women write differently if they thought their work was publishable, but their writing was affected by thoughts of imaginary and actual censors, which led some to write in code.

Traditionally, men have seen women's diaries as a threat. Women were said to be witches just because they kept them. Jane Carlyle wrote at the start of her 1855 journal, perhaps with thought of her essayist husband Thomas in mind, 'I remember Charles Buller saying of the Duchess of Praslin's murder, "What could a poor fellow do with a wife who kept a journal but murder her." There was a certain hidden truth in that light remark.' [15] Have husbands today smashed cameras and attacked photographers?

In 19th-century Britain, a diary could function as a way to keep Victorian women quiet and perhaps to display (marriageable) feminine virtues. Like creating seaweed albums or watercolour paintings, keeping diaries indicated gentility, sensitivity, ability to order 'nature'. It was not rumbustious. The constraints of the form may have driven such women insane. Other women, as Rozsika Parker points out in *The Subversive Stitch*, [16] may have covertly used the space to reflect, daydream or be creative.

In the mid-to-late 20th century, by contrast, some women have seen diaries as a place of freedom from external control, a place to try out new behaviour and ideas. American writer Anaïs Nin began writing journals in order to cope with her difficult teenage years and carried on – and on. [17] Psychoanalyst and writer Marion Milner is particularly useful because of her explorations into ways diaries can be used for therapy, including methods of working with the left and right side of the brain. [18] Jungian creative journal theorist/therapist Ira Progoff has been crucial in the lives of many women, including Jo Spence, for the ideas for journal-keeping which Tristine Rainer made accessible in *The New Journal*. [19] American writer May Sarton, on seeing how much she omitted her anger in a previous journal, set out deliberately to record it in *Journal of a Solitude*.

When is a diary more like a letter?

Other women, not published, were known and loved for the thoughts and feelings they expressed in letters rather than journals. Long, intimate, detailed letters functioned as a kind of diary to a guaranteed audience of at least one (the recipient) and maybe her family, the person who delivered the mail or nosy employers or employees.

Confining this chapter to the topic of journals is difficult, because some women's letters are so close in quality to diaries. Partly this is because of the expectations diary writers had of being read; partly because of the frankness with which letters can be written. Reading the pages of 19th-century Afro-American Charlotte Forten Grimke, [20] I had to keep checking whether these were diaries or letters. Their immediacy and intimacy suggested they could be either.

I'd like to propose a model that may work in some instances: a ring of concentric circles of honesty. It could be that the 'truest' things we write, or photograph, are in journals, because primarily that journal is for our purpose, not anyone else's. The next most 'honest' form may be letters or pictures taken for others, which we shape to some extent for the recipient. Then, finally, in that outer circle, there are memoirs, usually written or photographed much more retrospectively and with the expectation that they may be seen by women and men we will never meet.

In diaries, letters and photographs we present a version of ourselves which is partial. It leaves out bits of us that we think the reader or viewer might not want to know about, or that we may want to keep secret. The account has a specific frame. There may be no such simple unproblematic thing as the 'real truth about me' in a journal, letter or picture, just endless interesting versions of ourselves, different not only each moment but in each letter, journal page, poem or photograph.

I suspect that one reason working-class women didn't write diaries was for the same reason that they haven't taken photographs, even if they have the equipment: because of a sense that life wasn't worth recording. Therefore, letters home might have had the function not of recalling incidents and feelings as in a diary, but of reassuring those who might be worrying about us (and even of spinning a story to ourselves). It might have been true for Caribbean women moving to Britain in the 1950s, as it was for Sarah-Jane Metzger. In 1926, she came to London from the Rhymney Valley in south Wales to work, when she was 14 and a half.

> See, I left school when I was 13. Writing letters to my mum, that was different, but diaries – I think I thought I'd be hopeless at writing... No, I don't think any of the girls I knew wrote diaries; well, there wasn't the time... All the diaries are in your mind, isn't it, for us girls in service... See, we didn't have the money or time to go to museums or see things, so what could you write about? Only your job. And that was the same, day after day.
>
> We wrote to her every week, but we never told her how miserable we were. No. It was how wonderful it was, in London, because you didn't want to upset your mother. She didn't want us to come to London in the first place but it was that or starve. [21]

Her words suggest several reasons why some of the most marginalised women didn't and don't write diaries: unease about their level of literacy; the idea that entries wouldn't conform to the standard of interest expected of a diary writer; the stated lack of time.

How do we learn about marginalised women's lives then?

Post-1960s developments such as the Federation of Worker Writers and Community Publishers, creative writing classes, adult literacy initiatives, lesbian groups who publish their biographies and black women's groups all now suggest that women can indeed, as Amrit Wilson said of Asian women, 'find a voice'. [22] Similarly, access to a camera – however problematic the cost of film or daunting the posing/framing convention – can mean the finding of an eye, of a new and potent way to 'speak'.

Oral history has been particularly valuable in tracing the histories of working-class women who haven't created written or picture journals. But it does enable us to go back only to the last part of the 19th century.

In the last two decades there has been a strong move towards researching our roots. But because of the limitations to what can be unearthed, we may be forced to invent ideas of what might have been. Daughters and female descendants are the ones who usually do the poking around in the family history, remembering the stories and connections. And through gaining a feminist perspective on exclusion and hidden potential, we may well decide to fabricate histories of shadowy foremothers. This can be done lightheartedly or seriously, as Drusilla Beyfus did in *Poppy*. [23] This Australian writer fictionalised her mother's biography. She wrote as a daughter who didn't actually exist, and she invented a diary that didn't exist either, as a way to find out about a woman now dead and to pick up all the intuitions that can get left out of a conventional biography.

Conclusion

Diaries are invaluable for understanding women's history. They can also lead us to underestimate our history unless we look at them critically. Diaries written raw and immediately are far better than any hindsight account. But they are only one account of the truth. Letters, accounts of dreams, lies (such as stories and plays), are needed too. Photographs can be 'read' in conjunction with diaries, so that we can see how the external body behaviour denies, confirms, enhances the official account (for example, I can write in my diary that I felt quite grounded at Jo's funeral, whereas later snaps may show me smiling, embarrassed, biting my nails, hunching my shoulders). They can add to, comment on or contradict words. Yet they can be in their own right a valid means of articulating experience. Pictures can lie in the same way as words; they can be public or private; they are as open as words to interpretation, and they can be as structured by internalised conventions and knowledge.

A woman's gotta have a camera as well as a journal, as her

companion for the future. How else are our descendants going to find out about us?

Sources

1. Jo Spence, *Cultural Sniping: The Art of Transgression*, London, Routledge, 1995.
2. Edith Simcox, *Autobiography of a Shirt Maker*, Bodleian Library, Oxford, Ms Eng. Misc. d.494. Quoted in Chapter 3, 'Edith Simcox and Heterosexism in Biography: A Lesbian-Feminist Exploration' by Pam Johnson, in *Not Just a Passing Phase: Reclaiming Lesbians in History 1840–1985*, by the Lesbian History Group, London, Women's Press, 1989.
3. Tristine Rainer, *The New Journal*, London, Angus & Robertson, 1980, p.20.
4. Millicent Garrett Fawcett, large green Boer concentration camps album. Fawcett Library, London.
5. Marjory Lees, Diary of Oldham women's suffrage pilgrimage, ref. 2/OWS box 150. Fawcett Library, London.
6. Ruth First, *117 Days*, London, Bloomsbury, 1988.
7. Anne Frank, *The Diary of Anne Frank*, London, Hutchinson Educational, 1970.
8. Lady Sarashina, *As I Crossed the Bridge of Dreams: Recollections of a Woman in Eleventh Century Japan*, tr. Ivan Morris, New York, Dial, 1971. Also, Sei Shonagon, *The Pillow Book of Sei Shonagon*, tr. and ed. Ivan Morris, New York, Columbia Press, 1967.
9. T. Rainer, op.cit. p.19.
10. Doris Lessing, *The Golden Notebook*, London, Panther, 1973.
11. *Women's Work: Two Years in the Life of a Women Artists' Group (1983–85)*. Written and published by the Women's Work group, 1986.
12. Terry Dennett, 'Popular Photography and Labour Albums', in *Family Snaps* by Jo Spence and Patricia Holland, London, Virago, 1991.
13. British Women's Emigration Association 1885–1919. Cuttings scrapbooks 1/BWE. Also St Joan's Social and Political Alliance 1911–54. Scrapbooks. 2/sJP. Fawcett archive.
14. Autograph album, 1902, in Vida Goldstein boxes, Fawcett archives.
15. T. Rainer, op.cit. p.44. Jane Carlyle source not specified but almost certainly *Letters and Memorials of Jane Welsh Carlyle*, 3 vols. Prepared for publication by T. Carlyle, ed. James Froude, Longmans, Green, 1883.
16. Rozsika Parker, *The Subversive Stitch*, London, The Women's Press, 1986.
17. Anaïs Nin, Journals (5 vols. 1931–47), London, Quartet.
18. Marion Milner, *A Life of One's Own* (1986), *Eternity's Sunrise: A Way of Keeping a Diary* (1987), London, Virago.
19. T. Rainer, op.cit.
20. From the journal of Charlotte Forten Grimke, ed. Ray Allen Billington, New York, Collier, 1961, p.148–53. Quoted in *Black Women in White America*, ed. Gerda Lerner, London, Vintage, 1973, p.96.
21. Sarah-Jane Metzger, interview with author, 3 September 1992.
22. Amrit Wilson, *Finding a Voice*, London, Virago, 1978.
23. Drusilla Beyfus, *Poppy*, London, Serpent's Tail, 1990.

'you look all right to me'

D rawing was how it all began for me. It was all I did – tracing books, paint-by-number sets, colouring in books: the thatched cottage, the mare and foal, the clown. I coloured in other people's worlds. Mine was scary. I itched and scratched, I couldn't breathe properly and most of my time was spent in bed. It was NORMAL to me.

In 1951 my mother Gracie had given birth to a perfect golden curly-haired little girl. The little girl had 'inherited' eczema. It hurt to be touched. It hurt to be looked at – my arms, hands and legs in bandages. I scratched my way through childhood and soon became asthmatic. We lived in one room in my grandparents' council house in south-east London. All I could physically do was listen to Gracie reading to me, read fairy stories, write and draw. I laughed 'happily' in blissful ignorance. I had no idea that this wasn't EVERYONE's experience. I sat and watched and created my own world. I could be in control.

Forty years later I'm an artist and I'm still trying to take command of my unpredictable lungs, my blood pressure and my world. The only time I can honestly say I feel in control is when I'm creating something. In the past this has been through the activity of drawing: the decision-making, the power over every mark that goes down. Ultimate control of a world.

Working-class people spend their lives proving they're not stupid – working-class asthmatic lesbians don't have the breath! I was only ever interested in people, in trying to communicate with them. This was easier to do through drawing – it was all I knew. I could draw inaccessible, beautiful women and surround them with lots of space; I could make plaster casts of my close friends, take photographs of them and have them relate to each other. They are CAPTURED. The closeness will now ALWAYS be there. They are mine. I'm in control.

So drawing for me is totally self-engrossing and powerful but it does take time. I find photography gives me 'instant gratification' – instant images. For example, I set up portrait-type situations, select, repose, rephotograph, photocopy, manipulate 'accidental' images. It's a process of discovery, a visual diary – a record of what's happening to me as a woman with invisible disabilities. My work and the way in which I choose to work is, I've discovered, all part of my DIS-EASES, and my attempt at taking charge of them.

You look all right to me.

1953.

Fragile

I set out to investigate my childhood: I interrogated Gracie for her stories and her version of my young life. Despite the intense stress she was under trying to bring up an eczematic/asthmatic child with critical, judgemental in-laws in their house, and my dad working from 4.30 am every day, Gracie did a remarkably good job loving and nurturing me, and encouraging my talents and strengths. Her anecdotes were accompanied by visual 'evidence' from our family album. We concluded that I was shy, but happy and quite content to play on my own. I was intelligent, creative and capable. I also had asthma and allergies. I saw my main allergy as the world outside, which I soon discovered was NO SAFE PLACE. I was seen as a 'highly strung, over-protected invalid'. It wasn't until my thirties that I began to question this perception; to use photography as a

Fragile.

Family of carers.

The next breath?

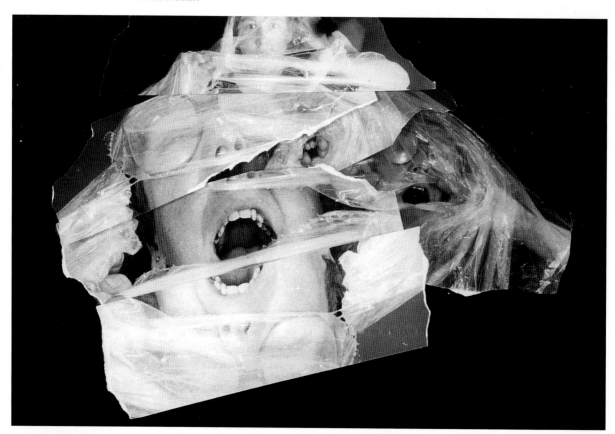

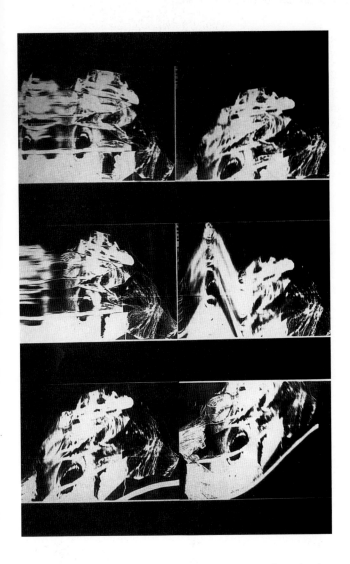

Status asthmaticus.

means of exploring my place in the world – a sort of self-help therapy, a process of confidence-building which was necessary after a bout of asthma. One of the characteristics of the disease is its unpredictability. I have to be totally dependent on a carer because attacks occur without warning, followed by the slow regaining of physical and emotional strength and control. I find it essential to have people around who are constant and calm. The strain and demands on relationships are therefore tremendous. I also need stimulation and excitement when I recover. I have a family of carers, but I also feel isolated.

Status asthmaticus
This body of work I made in 1988 in collaboration with a friend, Linda, who has witnessed the reality of my attacks. I wanted to show the terrifying struggle for the next breath. I wanted to express the feelings of suffocation I experience during an asthma attack,

The normal life of a 40-year-old.

the exhaustion, the panic, the sense of being totally out of control, the not knowing if THIS time I may not survive. The images are constructed, printed and distorted through a photocopier to show each stage of the attack. I've considered taking self-portraits during an actual attack, but my fear is that they are likely to be the last images of me, and I wouldn't want that! I still had to get these rather gruelling images off my chest. Now I want to move on, to draw more from other aspects of my personality, in particular, my humour. As I came to photography from a fine art and theatre design background, I'm more interested in producing images which please me and which will affect an observer. I see my images as having a bitter-sweet content. Although the subject matter is essentially serious, I present them in a humorous way: I like to play.

The normal life of a 40-year-old
Last year I achieved the age of 40. As a doctor handed me the supermarket shopping list which passes for a prescription, he said: 'There's no reason why you shouldn't live the NORMAL life of a 40-year-old.' Or was it the life of a NORMAL 40-year-old?

I smiled, for both descriptions were beyond my conception. What did they mean? I set out to investigate. To celebrate surviving that long, I took a series of portraits featuring some of the paraphernalia I've had to surround myself with in order to live my life to the best of my ability. The medications, the physical aids, herbal treatments, aromatherapy, massage and self-help therapy books – *The Asthmatic's Action Plan*. I'm still working, I'm still playing and I'm still taking pictures.

true to my potential

I was born in Johannesburg in 1970 to a 16-year-old girl and soon afterwards adopted. Sometimes I am asked whether having two mothers and two cultures has confused me and I must admit that when I was younger it did, especially as I am black and my mother is white.

Occasionally I wonder what it would have been like if my biological mother had kept me. Looking through some pictures recently, I found a picture of her (I left South Africa when I was four and have not seen her since), and a contemporary picture of myself. Out of curiosity I put the two together and was totally shocked to see how similar we look. It was the juxtaposition of two familiar pictures I'd had around that led me to this insight.

It makes me angry that I should resemble her at all. When I least expect it I remember things from my childhood in South Africa, but

Mother and daughter who are strangers.
An uneasy similarity for me.

My biological mother, Tiny, my brother Rubin and me. One of the few times we were together.

until now my past has come trickling into my life in the shape of snapshots, evoking jarring feelings of ambivalence. Unexpectedly, my biological mother will write to me assuming the tone of 'mother'. This makes me feel very angry, invaded and guilty for having these feelings. Ultimately, I know deep down in my heart that I owe it to myself and her to go and meet her, but the thought of going frightens me.

Being a young woman is such a pain. I am constantly surrounded by images which dictate that thin and long-legged is beautiful and the amount of pressure I feel to conform to this ideal is unbelievable. The knowledge that I come from a culture that prizes plump women does not help at all. I force myself into clothes that do not suit me and I get upset. I find my solace in eating and consequently get caught up in a vicious circle. I have an image in my head of what I should look like that persecutes me, but I haven't the perseverance to achieve it. Perhaps I know that my build makes it an unrealisable goal.

Student social life, revolving as it does around drinking, does not help with my weight. I feel enormous peer-group pressure to fit in. We push one another to drink a lot, so 90 per cent of my social life is spent in a state of blurred euphoria. A 'good time' is expensive, but is it a good time? Not really. We make no contact and I am left lonely.

Paradoxically, part of my problem is the considerable amount of money I earn as a waitress. This enables me to indulge in one of my biggest loves – shopping. Another form of feeding myself. A great deal of my energy and money goes on my appearance. It is as if I need to hide behind a smart exterior. I know that my clothes do not portray who I am, but they influence how other people perceive me.

**Students policing themselves in order
to avoid drunken brawls.**

The lynchpin of student social life.

I used to cultivate different images, but now I present myself as smart and unapproachable. It gives me a sense of control – a total illusion, I know.

I wish belonging to a group did not matter and that I could redirect my energy. My social life and waitressing are taking precedence over my academic work. It's not that my work isn't interesting, but I am not a major academic. Often I feel that I am drowning in books, so I go out. The pressure to do well does not only come from my parents, but from knowing that as a black woman I have to do better than most. I am afraid of failure. If I do not try then I cannot fail. Maybe I should never have embarked on a degree. My grades are good, but nothing spectacular.

Working on this article has helped me to identify and work with the problems I have in order to try to understand them. I have never enjoyed having my picture taken so I was hesitant about going ahead. There has always been a struggle inside me about photography. When I was 12 my mother gave me an Olympus OM10 for Christmas. I never used it. I felt that Mum would take over whatever I did with my camera as she is a professional photographer. Through doing this piece I finally began to understand what she had hoped for in giving me my camera. She wanted share with me her passion for photography.

Several real surprises have emerged from doing this work. How powerful it has been using my camera to explore myself visually – what a chameleon I am! I see the potential for using pictures to create a journal: how quickly they jog the memory and bring floods of associations that make moments of my life really vivid, for instance, all the student pictures that I have; how putting seemingly

The things I do to try to look more attractive. But in the end all I am left with are the products, which cannot really change me anyway.

The smart, bubbly girl everyone sees socially.

Sometimes the pressure is too much and I wonder what I am doing.

unrelated images together brings sudden and for me disturbing insights. In the process of working on this project I have learned that you can actually use a camera to relate to someone. And the control I was looking for in manipulating my clothes? Well, I took complete control of this whole project and it was I who said how all my images should be.

claire collison

do they mean me?

I originally learned how to use a camera in order to give a shape to the sensation I had of never recognising myself in the images of women that surrounded me, a 'do they mean me?' sort of emotion that reached fever pitch when I was working as a life model and became reduced to an abstract female form. This taking control, getting inside the icon and subverting it, was, in retrospect, a personal form of phototherapy.

Photography means 'painting with light'. For me it is not a captured moment, but something staged. I make photos rather than take them. Some are loyal reproductions of a picture in my mind's eye; others have changed and grown out of an idea through improvisation or accident. I make them because I have to. They occupy a space where words will not do. They are not intended as illustrations of theory. I hope to trigger an emotional response, a recognition and out of that perhaps a curiosity. I can't 'explain' them, but I can describe my reasons for making them and provide the technical (I use the word loosely) information. The techniques are merely tools to be used.

My mum had given me a camera for my 21st birthday (a Minolta X500 – I wanted one that could be used completely manually). I enrolled at the local night class. Nightmare! Silver halide crystals, big lenses and 'Which lovely lady would like to pose for us this week?' All gadgets and trousers. I fled while I could still remember what it was I wanted to do. The local adult education centre was better; I was given access to equipment and help when asked for. But as my work became more private I felt uncomfortable watching my images emerge out of the developer rubbing shoulders with dodgy glamour shots. I needed somewhere more private. I set up a darkroom in my flat.

Do It Yourself (1987) is about autonomy.

How: **I set the camera on a tripod with cable release and also time release (you tend to get a constipated expression with the squeeze on cable release; also the few seconds of 'beep-beep' allow for the possibility of theatre).**
Where: **My bedroom floor**
Light: **From window**
The benefit of placing objects on the floor and leaving a space to leap in, apart from the weird effect it has on perspective, is being able to frame the composition in the viewfinder.

Not Ophelia, 1987.

Photographed in the same way. The plastic flowers were tinted later. I'd recently finished studying English and drama and was frustrated by the lack of opportunity there had been for real creativity, and appalled at the scarcity of decent roles for women, especially ones who didn't go mad, or drown, or both.

The Godmother and **Milky Way**,
1988.

Part of a piece called *Imaging the
Future*. I was exploring the science-
fiction subject of the perfect female
form and reproduction, looking at
the 'virgin and mother' double
standards applied to women. I'd
spent some time living with my mum
in Granada, and couldn't help but
notice the contrast between these
passive, bleeding, weeping,
lactating Dolorosas and my very
mortal madre! I was also concerned
with the 'fiction of science' – how
technology and legislation have
tried to render women invisible in
the process of baby-making.

How: **The milk bottles were hung
from skypoles with fishing wire (a
wayward one spinning in the wrong
direction was burned out in the
printing). I sprinkled demerara sugar
on the paper before exposing it, so it
is a photograph and photogram
combined.**

I've begun to realise how lucky I am not to have had any formal training in photography. Not knowing the rules, I was unaware of breaking them. I've had the freedom to make it up as I go along. My home-made methods owe a nod of thanks to *Blue Peter*, B movies and *Bunty*.

In 1988 I collapsed, fell asleep for two days, and discovered I had developed ME (myalgic encephalomyelitis). The next work I produced was in 1990 as part of 'Silent Health', commissioned by Camerawork.

Working on this project was a turning-point in my experience of ill health. As I had started to understand that a period of severe stress and overwork had contributed to my susceptibility to ME, my response for the previous 18 months had been to stop doing anything I had done that would use up my energy. My body had started to give out quite dramatic signals to that effect (amongst other things, I had become allergic to photographic chemicals), so I abandoned my darkroom until I 'got well again' and tried to learn to do nothing. Like anyone who had enjoyed averagely good health, my experience of illness was primarily one of losing control. My interpretation of post-1980s feminism had been an independence that meant the need for no one, and this was reflected in the way I had used photography. Using self-portrait-based images meant I had megalomaniac control of all parts of the process from pose to print. As I was no longer able to work in this manner, I felt I was no longer able to work.

After a lifetime's conditioning to judge myself by what I'd achieved, it was not only difficult but also unhealthy to try to switch to this inactivity. The chance of working on a topic as close to my heart as women and health came just in time.

To begin with, I had imagined I'd still be able to produce the pictures of my mind's eye only by delegating the parts of the process I was unable to do myself. I didn't foresee the problems that would arise from the fundamental loss of control; the need to ask, to communicate, and to end up with images that were not exactly the ones I had planned. This is not an apology for the photos I ended up with, but the lesson I didn't realise I was learning – that a different way need not be a compromise, that I still control the idea and that being forced by necessity to explore different methods might even strengthen rather than dilute the original.

The photos were an exploration of doing versus being; of where energy seeps to when you're not looking; of the contradictory pressures that tug at us and shape us despite ourselves, and of the uneasy relationship we have with our bodily functions. They were a chance to make visual an illness that is usually met with the response 'But you don't look ill,' and empowering in validating my experience of an illness whose very existence is questioned by some. I dedicated them to any woman who thought she was invincible.

Sweating, 1990.

One of the many symptoms of ME is sweating – profound, racehorse-like night sweats. It was important to learn to accept this as a positive process: my body flushing out toxins. I started to think about sweating, a bodily function that although non-gender-specific signifies contrary things when applied to men and women. Sweat and sex. Horses sweat, men perspire, women glow. I wanted to 'positive-image' sweating by turning myself into a classical fountain. The technique is by way of a homage to the Cottingley Fairies. It tickles me that two girls aged ten and 15, with a borrowed camera, some painted cardboard and a hatpin, pulled off such a great scam as convincing the world that there were fairies at the bottom of the garden. But it could be said that this hoodwinking, which exploited our absolute faith in photographic truth, and had us believe in the reality of a myth, was the prototype advertisement. Which brings us back to the pressure not to sweat. How: A black and white print of me, cut out with the edges painted, held slightly out of focus in front of tiny waterfall in the park (fingers in shot by way Brechtian demystification!).

Charity, 1990.

Eight times more women than men have ME, and a large percentage of those come from the caring professions (so much for Yuppie 'flu...). I wanted to consider the stresses that were more likely to affect women, from childhood expectations to the nurturing roles traditionally placed on us.

Selfishness, 1990.

I made the series *Faith*, *Hope* and *Charity*, literally projecting images on to myself. Selfishness is meant as an antidote to the selflessness of the traditional virtues, to affirm the goodness of loving yourself; you can't afford to wait to be endorsed – or bought flowers – so treat yourself!

Peeling Potatoes in Paradise/Mustn't Waste Time, 1990.

It is ironic that I was compelled to make an image about the need to learn to do nothing.

How: **Cut-out model with potatoes graded in size from Cyprus new to King Edwards. I projected a slide of clouds over everything.**

Reconciliation, 1990.

Nicked from Burne Jones' *Pygmalion*. I'd always loved the painting and hated the story. I wanted to make a landmark image of acceptance – embracing my weaknesses, distinguishing between spiritual and physical strength, realising that getting better was different from returning to how I was before I was ill.

How: **Pressing down the rewind button on the bottom of camera whilst holding the rewind crank, wind on. Take a second exposure. Of 36, this is the only one where I'm not hugging my knees, or worse. Expect to waste a lot of film.**

Glands Like Marbles, 1992.

This is about the once-removed sense of ourselves with which the medicalising of any condition leaves us, and the fetishising that must occur when we talk about the ill 'bits' of our bodies. My glands have become my early-warning system, and literally become hard as marbles when I've been overdoing things. I heard a woman describe her shoulder ache as like 'a wardrobe dragging on gravel'. I have great respect for the numbskull school of body-speak.

How: **A slide of marbles was projected over my torso. I wore long black gloves to absorb the projection. The slide image made me feel quite dressed and protected.**

Fresh Fruit and Foreign Places, 1992.

I have shoeboxes full of photos which aren't of the meditative, constructed style that I exhibit, but are a spontaneous glad-to-be-alive gobbling up of the joy of looking. The felicias that make the border of this came out of one of those shoeboxes. It was a milestone for me to not feel the need for any theoretical justification beyond 'a little bit of what you fancy does you good'.

How: **I used a £5 reversal ring to turn my 50mm lens into a macro for the flowers. The central image is taken using a *Top of the Pops*-style prism lens (also a fiver).**

left *Pretty Baa Lambs*

below *From Pre-Raphaelite Brotherhood to Pre-menstrual Sisterhood*, 1993.

A version-excursion of Ford Maddox Brown's painting *Pretty Baa Lambs*, from the Birmingham Museum and Art Gallery collection, which was commissioned as part of the Billboard Project (Birmingham) and exhibited on a 10x20-foot hoarding in April 1993. With most of the work I'd done prior to this, I hadn't felt the need to censor myself as I had ensured that my work would only be seen in 'safe' environments and in a specific context. With this project I endeavoured to produce an image that defied misappropriation. I cast aside my Luddite misgivings and entered the Nineties by using computer magic to combine my photographic mock-up with the painting. This part of the process I talked into existence, having someone – Philip King – with the technical expertise to realise my ideas for me. To either side of the main image were huge blow-up photos of plastic chops, and the frame was covered with synthetic grass and plastic flowers. I wanted to explore notions of fine art and advertising, and culture and nature. It seems that over 140 years not much has changed. The unattainability of a dream still makes it no less desirable. Ford Maddox Brown's 'perfick' landscape no more existed in his day than the thatched cottage or paradise island does in ours (he created his pastoral in Stockwell, I mine in Brixton). Women and nature do not combine as comfortably as they would appear to do in this Laura Ashley vision of life, but they are united in the way they are similarly exploited. I wanted this piece to be about the crass second-hand experience we accept as 'natural' – the pine disinfectant and rose air freshener, and the latest rash of adverts proclaiming the greenness of their products, which is sadly more a cynical manipulation of public concern than genuine change.

I leave the final word to my critics, as represented by a note in the comments book for 'One Girl's Adventure' (Exeter, 1992): 'Since 1972 I have seen many examples of narcissistic photographs of young women but this is probably the best example of the genre I have seen.'

i couldn't waste my camera

A woman with a camera.

The Swing

A swing goes in and out,
Up and down.
It goes, and goes, and goes,
Only the swinger knows
Her dreams flow in rhythm,
And her body works her mind,
To find
The depth,
Or height of her mood.
She is suspended in her own space,
Going to and fro,
Getting nowhere,
Yet reaching out to every place,
From rope, and seat, and angle,
With freedom
To work, or dream, or dangle.

My urge to take photographs had a very shaky start. I'm not in the least technical (I've never really got the hang of using a steam iron). Apart from this, I'm addicted to justifying the cost of everything. However, about six years ago my son gave me a brand-new camera. I couldn't waste it. Now my very own camera is truly a part of me – or rather, of the new me.

The brief for this book was 'My life as it is now – warts and all – plus a picture from my past.' The past is in fact my future. I am 60 years old, a mother of three and a grandmother. I had an elementary education and am now best described as a late starter.

I've coupled the snap of feet with my poem 'The Swing' for a special reason. The feet belong to some members of our women's writers group. Ours is not just a workshop, it's a place that truly encapsulates trust, hope, understanding, humour and encouragement. It's a special kind of female freedom. Some of us also belong to mixed workshops. I wrote 'The Swing' about eight years ago.

Thoughts about shopping have now ceased to drown my mind. This empty spiral staircase near our local supermarket gives me more satisfaction than the miles of well-stocked shelves.

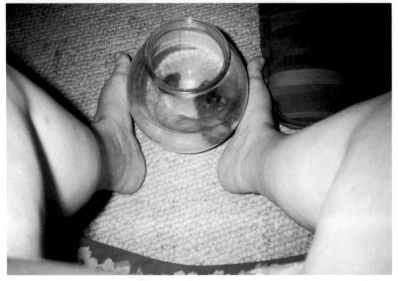

I don't quite live alone. I have a 12-year-old goldfish called Desmond. My daughter won him at the fair. He is very knowing and welcomes me home. He likes a cuddle, or should I say a tickle. Hands and feet are the same to him.

I saw this note on the end of an information pack on photography: 'What you see through the viewfinder is more important than anything else.' I've coupled this lesson with the slow realisation that at long last I can recognise myself. Not for what I want to be, but for what I am. A woman with a camera.

In looking through my viewfinder I've sort of framed my own life. I've reminded myself that family ties are very tight. They go on forever, each member patiently waiting for all those promised tomorrows. A strange sort of self-portrait has slowly been squeezed out of my tube of existence, a constructed montage of reality and symbolic forms created with my own inner eye – held in my hands in the form of my very own camera. I keep thinking about butterflies and the people who pin them out for display or shut them away in beautifully made, slim drawers.

Those still objects are a bit like my 'snaps'. They too are blank on the reverse side. My camera has held time still on a sheet of blank paper. No morphine bottle, just a pen of light. So what does the back of my head tell you about me? And my mind?

The true realisation of being behind the scenes dawned through another medium as well when I heard my own words being acted out by young actors. In writing plays I took on a whole new world of observation.

Women who have to swear on the bible saying, 'This is the truth, the whole truth and nothing but the truth,' will understand the utter despair and degradation that goes on in your mind about what you are having to swear as true. It is a real situation that you and your husband and children have to live with, yet try so hard to pretend isn't true. Bruises fade; court photos don't. Neither do they go into the family album. Your eyes tell you, 'This is true. This is the proof.' But your heart tells you not to believe, leaving you to slowly become your own compost heap.

Photo: Avon & Somerset County Constabulary

the family: inside closed doors

woman in exile

The Blue Guitar

They said, 'You have a blue guitar,
You do not play things as they are.'

The man replied, 'Things as they are
Are changed upon the blue guitar.'

Wallace Stevens

My family album looks basically like most others. There are groups of people smiling, at parties, at the beach, sightseeing on holidays, essentially at play. It is full of moments I would never want to disown. But there is more to this story. Apart from this official family album, my workroom burgeons with photographs. I have them on every surface and taking a closer look at these and the family album, I think of lines from Wallace Stevens' poem 'The Blue Guitar'.

Some of my pictures are in frames, like that of my mother's six brothers standing in a row, all dead now but one, or like the one of my sister posing, formal and beautiful, in her new flat, no hint of her painful divorce; a loved aunt, long since dead, in a fancy art-deco frame far too big for the stern little black and white print. Others are just propped against walls or books. I keep moving my pictures around. Meanings shift and change. New patterns of family relationships emerge, but never is everything revealed.

Take the picture that stands amid the paraphernalia on my desk. It is one of my favourite pictures of my daughter Joyce. It was taken by a school photographer and I love looking at it. She is wearing a new uniform, her first, and is very proud of it. Her smile is sweet, shy and amused, and on her head, tying the little top-knot, whirls her ribbon like a tiny propeller. The holes that puncture her lobes are empty. I know she had lost her earrings. For mothers, looking affectionately at school photographs, meaning goes far beyond the surface image. From this photograph what would anyone else know about Joyce? Her image is there, but her reality remains hidden. Who would know, for instance, that I fell in love with Joyce when she was six days old, a velvety petal of a child with seed-pearl toes, or that I was lucky enough to be entrusted with caring for her? No one could tell that she is the oldest child in her natural family and the youngest in mine. Her complex history is too big a burden for one photograph. This picture and many others act as mines of memory waiting to be excavated, to reveal truths about the sitter and often about the photographer. A whole collection of family photographs is but the tip of an iceberg; a hidden nine tenths is there to be amplified.

How could snapshots, fractions of seconds frozen in time, ever yield up all their meaning? We make our own sense of pictures in the way we use them to tell our stories. Yet when we begin to tug at that dense tangle that is 'I', the images we want are missing.

There's one important one from my childhood which I wish I had. Imagine a strip of lawn where a small white girl sits enraptured by the black man beside her who plucks at a stringed instrument the shape of a huntsman's bow. Between the faraway songs he plays come the faraway stories he tells her each night till bedtime. No one in my family would have thought of taking such a picture, though when the family snapping sessions did happen, he, Jack, was in them too. Who was Jackson Mbowene? He was the man who worked for my parents. He was my childhood mother, father and friend whose endless stories and agile fingers picking intricate rhythms on his home-made stringed gourd taught me how a herd boy, son of a famed witch-doctor, grew up to be a servant. I learned to love African music and I learned to become an exile in what I later found out to be a fiercely racist country. There are levels of exile. Feeding on Jack's culture I learned to be an exile in my own family as I guess do many children in their rich fantasy life. Perhaps we are all exiles from the norms presented to us.

Neither is there an image of an early moment of paradise, nor my exile from it. But there's a 'thought feeling' snapshot in my head. I am lying on a divan with my back against the wall, sun pouring through the large window opposite. I am looking into the black and cherry red checks of my mother's woollen dress. She lies with her back to me and I am stroking her. I am loving my space between her and the wall and the feel of the warm soft wool. Why was she lying down during the day? Was she pregnant with my sister? The spare room, where we were, would become my room when my sister was born. In fact the very night she was born I was put there screaming, barred from my mother (who was probably in labour in the next room) by Auntie Ethel, who was totally deaf to my night-long screams and who, kindly soul, I hated for the rest of her life.

I peer at old family snaps. It's difficult to read anything about this child who was myself, mostly scowling at the camera or very solemn, with the exception of one vividly contrasting picture taken on the beach with some of my aunts (not Ethel) and my cousins. I am grinning radiantly, quite coherent with what I vaguely remember of those long sunny days on the beach, careless and vibrantly happy. Summer in South Africa really was always sunny and the sea, for which I've retained an abiding passion, always intensely blue. Was my mother taking that picture? She's not in it and my father never came on holiday with us. His absence and the reason for it is something you can't read from a snapshot. How do you photograph 'never having had a holiday'? My father could never afford it. When his work restarted after the war, he would do overtime to enable us to go to the seaside, where we'd stay with my mother's family. The trio of my mother, sister and myself appears often in our family album. In this tableau I'm either staring tight-lipped and separate, or holding my dress in some pretty pose. What is happening inside this child?

Complex worlds are already spawned. Already I am split into several subject positions. I'm Jack's little mate, Mummy's pretty, clever girl, Daddy's chum and the 'other'. The 'other' I have been trying to uncover over the years.

With my father I am his Sunday-morning friend. Some 'thought pictures' here. I am standing beside a glass showcase being told how wonderful it is to have hands that could make such glorious cakes, knit such intricate patterns. It is my father enthusing over these marvels. We're at the annual agricultural show and each year his excitement would carry me from the genius of some farming implement, through the fineness of a prize sheep to his 'Blimey, that's what you call hand-knitting.' My mother had taught me to knit before I started school and when I was ten the first-prize gold label, like the kind that hung round the necks of prize bulls, lay in the glass case of the children's section next to the butterfly-patterned jersey I had made. I don't remember what happened to the gold label or the jersey, but my father's 'by Joves' lie unfaded in the folds of my memory. He was proud, too, of the wonderful theatre costumes my mother designed and made, all through the night in those times during the war when paper was hard to come by and my father, a printer, had no work. He'd help with the cutting of those endless fantasy garments that filled our house. We were walking companions, too, my dad and I, taking our walks through the urban streets of Johannesburg some four miles or so to the zoo and back. I'm the assistant who takes my turn winding the ice-cream churn for Sunday's dessert (I can taste that custardy ice-cream now), or I'm called upon to hold planks of wood while he saws. I'm his son, the elder girl whom Freud claims is always a son in the family. But no son I, I was my father's Jewish daughter, barred from sitting beside him in the synagogue when I was 12. Women sit upstairs. The only reason I'd gone in the first place was to have my father to myself, so I was lost to the synagogue and my father stopped going as well. When on the rare occasion I have heard a Friday-night Shabbat service since then, it has sent tears

coursing down my face. It's my father I cry for.

Though I'm an exile from Judaism, its cultural values still inform my life. A passion for education took my cousins into the professions, out of their working-class backgrounds, and I went too. In terms of family relations the cost has been high. My mother was caught between being proud of me and feeling she'd lost contact with this daughter who was 'too intellectual', and I was double-bound in her pride and disparagement. Intoxicated by the worlds I'd discovered in Chaucer, Shakespeare, Spenser, Milton, Yeats, Whitman, I'd deny flatly and absolutely, with hot indignant tears, that I was an 'intellectual'. If that was a bad thing to be and it took me away from her love, then I was not it.

I turn back to the family album. None of this pain is visible there. What I find are numerous pictures of me as a dancer. Reviews, cuttings, examination results, all carefully stored together with endless pictures of me as a tiny tot, as a child, as a member of the ballet company. I'm a performer. Waves of recognition and nausea swamped me when I read *The Drama of Being a Child* by Alice Miller. It was like having my childhood laid bare. So this was it. Here, then, was the exile from myself. I can see my mother in the wider framework of her own deprivation, one of 12 siblings and often humiliated by older brothers. I see her seeking admiration and validation through her children, experiencing them not as the centre of their own activity, but as part of hers. She needs the accolades she won through me. Beyond this performing self I could not be heard. My dark, chaotic emotional self, that 'other' I mentioned earlier, was silent. Using my camera to make it visible, I have staged the 'scenes' of this emotional absence achieving, with this disclosure, a kind of cathartic acknowledgement of the child I never was. This muzzled and buried 'other' I toil to drag into the light.

It took a while to go on this inner journey. When I first became an immigrant in Britain in the 1970s, I was concerned with the whole issue of reflecting this multi-cultural British society in children's books. My daughter Joyce was five and ready for school. She makes friends easily and soon Ahmed and Gloria and Vinod and Musi were trickling home to tea. Fresh from the strictures of 'apartheid', this group of children made me bubble with pleasure. Now, where were the books that reflected this multi-cultural gang? My search took me to shelves of books reflecting middle-class white children and the trappings of their lifestyle. I discovered no books whatsoever for children who were not white. How, I asked myself, do Hindu and Muslim and Greek and West Indian children make sense of their experience in this society when representation of their families, habits, festivals, religions, in short their culture, is simply not there? Shifts of perception must confuse all small

opposite

The family snaps.

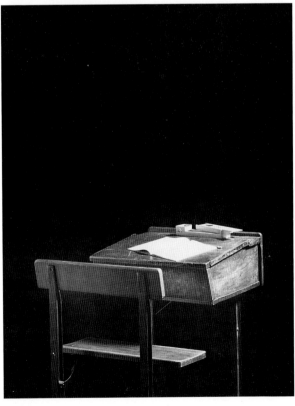

children when they leave what is familiar at home to face the strangeness of school. Imagine the bewilderment of a child whose mother wears a sari and eats with her fingers finding that in this new environment that is not how it is done at all. What do children do in these circumstances? Hide; become defensive on behalf of families who behave differently; feel shame and anger towards them for not measuring up and even more anger towards those who make them appear not to? How, I asked myself yet again, could reading mean anything at all when you never saw yourself in a book? Books had to be made. Using a camera to avoid the stereotypes which my poor illustrating would have produced, children, their families, teachers, a colleague and myself made books. In simple stories depicting cultures which differ from each other and in spaces where all children exist; in disappointments, delights, quarrels, resentments, lost teeth, found friends and play, they could find themselves and become owners of their own social kingdom. Books did not have to be for someone else. (Nor in the last resort do children need to be represented by anyone other than themselves. They take wonderful pictures and, with a little help, can make their own books.)

Through writing about and photographing the lived experience of children in minority groups, I would, I thought, enable them to identify with what was familiar in their lives. Indirectly, I realise I was dealing with the whole issue of my own upheaval. While endeavouring to reach realities of children across cultures, I was struggling to find a foothold in a new culture myself. It was new, but second-handedly familiar. England was 'home' to my mother, who lived her whole life in South Africa. The fabric of my growing up was a weave of Sunday roasts, bubble and squeak, treacle pudding; and proteas, jacarandas, papaya and mangos. Now I had lost the proteas and the wide skies, so blue in the day and laced in the endlessly clear nights with constellations that I knew so well. My identity was at stake. Now I needed my camera to help me probe and reveal feelings, to become my divining rod.

A coda
'We cannot theorise the workings or nature of remembering without at the same time considering the systematic mechanisms of forgetting. Once we begin to think of both seeing and memory as primarily defensive and self-protective operations, saturated with fantasy, then the status of photographic imagery is affected rather radically.' Simon Watney

Photographing can, per se, be defensive and self-protective. For the last five years of their lives, my parents, who died in their nineties, lived in an old people's home. They were frail and helpless. I used my camera like a person possessed, turning it towards what cut me

Creating the self.

Proteas and passports: exit and re-entry.

to the quick. I had to record my parents' ebbing lives, every detail of their room and their monumental daily struggle. I needed to record that vanishing present, to keep it and in some magical way keep my parents. The bundle of photographs I have, unbearably poignant and private, takes on new meanings. Grieving is a kind of rite of passage, another process of exile, a letting go of something I cannot in reality go back to.

I closed my mother's blue eyes with kisses when she died in my arms. The wonderful smile that lit so unexpectedly on my father's beautiful old face never appeared again. He died five days later. Almost two centuries' worth of life had vanished with my parents. Of those last few days, the only images that were finally recorded were those burned into the retinas of my eyes, branded there more intensely than they could have been on any film.

The most recent snapshot to go into my family album is one that I am including here. It's a symbol of me reclaiming my body, from which I was exiled for two painful years on crutches, having broken my hip after an accident on my bicycle. I can also use this image as another way of looking at those other exiles: from country, class, culture and family. Here I am flying, parasailing, it is called, and I am connected, though you cannot see it, to a boat which pulls me, while the parachute holds me aloft. The story I tell myself now is of those ropes, the connections holding me to culture, class, country, family and parents, all internalised, enabling me to inch my way back in memory to the dense fabric that lets me float free. I read recently of a fuchsia cutting 'tended by five generations of women, in the gardens of four counties, for more than a 100 years'. What heritage! Nothing like that can I claim, but if I cannot be anchored that securely, at least I can float securely. There is still much to be done in 'the foul rag-and-bone shop of the heart' to transform the former public me into an ageing me whose losses, liberating in one sense, can help to get me airborne and help to let 'the chaos and the sunlight' in. Who knows what direction I'll take? Perhaps I can hand on to my granddaughter (who slipped into my heart, a 2lb thread of life... another love affair, another story) at least the knowledge of choices and possibilities, and though I cannot give her roots, I can help her be aware of wings, and I can let her know that I have known the magical moments of flying.

clarissa sligh

These constructed photographs were made during the period 1984 to 1988. Except for *Play With Jane,* which is a serigraph, they are all van Dyke or brown prints, which is an alternative photographic process. During this period, I focused on deconstructing my identity as a 'raised poor southern Baptist female Negro American' and the inverse hegemonic myth of 'raised middle-class and owning-class American Caucasians'.

He was her husband when they played "HOUSE".

Played House, 1984.

Played House was the first constructed photograph. After spending nine months sketching one self-portrait daily, I pulled out my family photograph album and this image of me as a young person struck me the most. It seemed to capture everything about me as an adult. When one first looks at the image, one thinks of 'family outing' or something similarly sentimental. Yet the girl's look seems to say 'What do you want of me? Will I be able to figure it out?'

Surrounded by all those children, she looked directly at the camera, and appears very wary, serious, and sad. Under that childlike stillness there is a lot of anger. Of course, I am only able to say all this in hindsight – ten years after I made the image. It is amazing that the image speaks to me with such clarity about a reality that I could not face when I made it. This seems to happen all the time.

She Slept With Her Brother, 1984.
I think it's about early sexual memories
and learning internalised sexism.

Waiting For Daddy, 1987.

Re-enter the frame of the family. Replay
the moment. Recover the voice of the
youngest person in the photo and have it
direct the narrative. Re-evaluate that lost
human power, intelligence and clarity.

***Play With Jane,
1988.***
**The first image
made around the
reconstruction of
the education of
the 'Negro
American'.**

What's Happening With Momma? 1987

It was fall in Virginia.
Red and yellow leaves fell from tall oak trees.
As oak was the colour of Skookie's skin, she blended right
 in.
With the help of her two older brothers
she made a set of acorn pipes.

She sat under the trees play-acting 'Smoking like Daddy'.
When he lit up, it meant he was in a very good mood!
Now the sweet aroma of his tobacco smelled in her head.

As she sat daydreaming,
a loud piercing scream came from her momma's bedroom.
A dull thump sounded like someone had hit the floor.
Skookie jumped and ran into the house.

She saw her momma lying on the floor
It scared and confused her.
Slowly her momma's eyes opened.
'Go get your grandma!' she cried.
Stunned, Skookie ran out of the house
as fast as her legs could take her.

Just then her big brother Carl came around the corner.
He was coming home from school.
She screamed and hollered as she ran to him.
Snot and tears ran down her face.

The towering 14-year-old boy could tell
something was not right.
'What's wrong with you?' he demanded.
She could not stop crying.

Grasping at his sweater with one hand,
she pointed at the house with the other.
He pulled away and vaulted up the steps.
She ran behind him.
He came out of the bedroom, just as she got there.

As he ran out of the yard, he heard her footsteps behind
 him.
He did an about-face and ordered,
'Go back and stay in the house!'
She froze on the spot and watched him disappear from
 sight.
Her legs felt like wooden pegs.

Inside the house, her momma's screams
and moans of agony flowed through the walls.
Minute after minute dragged on.
Skookie's face and hands pressed against the cool window
 pane.
Her seven-year-old body began to tremble and shake.

Her grandma came.
She was holding four-year-old baby brother's hand tightly.
'Stay with your sister,' she said firmly as
she pushed him toward her.
Moving swiftly, she went in the bedroom and closed the
     door.

'Something awful must be wrong,' thought Skookie.
Memories of being a flower girl at Baptist funerals
raced through her mind.
She wrapped her arms around herself.
Crouched in the corner, she began rocking back and forth.

It was getting dark when the doctor and some neighbours
     came.
They gave Skookie quizzical looks as
they tried to act as if nothing was happening.

The small house became crowded.
Skookie wanted to leave, but she was too scared.
And where would she go?
Both of her big brothers were gone!

Her daddy arrived with a big bag of groceries.
The neighbours murmured in hush-hush tones.
Then Grandma spoke with him. She sounded very stern.

He went in the kitchen and fixed their dinner.

WHAT'S HAPPENING WITH *MOMMA?*

Baby brother would not eat.
Skookie throwed hers all up.
Angrily he yelled, 'If you don't eat I'm going to tear you
      up!'
They both began to cry.

Just then, Aunt Nana came out of her momma's room.
She looked at Skookie and asked,
'Do you know you have a new baby sister?'
Skookie's wet eyes clung to her face as she asked,
'How did a baby get there?'

Grinning widely she replied, 'The stork brought her!'
This didn't make any sense to Skookie.
'What's wrong with my momma?' she asked in
      a quivering voice.
'Your momma's going to be all right,' said Aunt Nana.

Still it was a bit too much!
Skookie's body collapsed into the chair as
her mind closed itself down for the night.
She did not know it yet but as big sister, she had become a
      mother!

Reframing the Past, 1988.
Placing the 'Negro American' family
snapshots within the stream of words
used to teach the 'Negro American'
child to read, to speak, to think, to act,
to hope, to be.

Wonderful Uncle, 1984–88.
An image created in an attempt to
capture the isolation and confusion
that sets in when a child is
confronted with being the target of
adult sexual desire. After making this
photograph, I became conscious of
the reality that a mother's reaction to
her daughter's dilemma is based more
on what has already happened to the
mother as a young person than on the
situation in which the daughter finds
herself.

memento mori manifest: a rite of inheritance

Reviewing

Fading fragments,
traces almost lost,
I turn these fragile pages
in search of you.

Who is this young man
I never knew?
This playful young couple
'Brighton pier and on board.'

Only a piece of paper
I hold now,
a certificate of presence,
I know only
that has been.

Your gaze fixed by chemicals,
I can no longer touch you,
change your expression
by my interactions.

I have now, only the evidence
that one day, in the garden,
you held me, protectively,
when I first learned to stand
on my own two feet,
and walk
away from you.

'It is the image in the mind that binds us to our lost treasures, but it is the loss that shapes the image.' Colette

I reach down the utility cardboard suitcase from the top shelf of the wardrobe in the boxroom and find it again. The leather binding is disintegrating, the photos tiny and faded to sepia, some now barely there at all. I had always been entranced by this particular family album, containing photographs of my parents when they were courting, aged 16 and 20. Who were that laughing couple on the beach at Felixstowe and Brighton? Who was that young man, with his carefully studied resemblance to current matinee idols, always posing, in every image, with cigarette in hand? My father was said to look like Ronald Colman, and wore that self-same neat moustache, so fashionable in the Thirties, all his life.

In 1986, I'm checking for evidence. In every picture, at least up till the 1960s, he is smoking.

Later, much later, in 1990, I am searching for something unique to him, something 'essential' of that particular man, my father. But, of course, it cannot be there. The closest I come to it is the recognition of his ability to encapsulate the style of his times, through the clothes he designed and made, the poses he struck and his selection of snapshots.

How is an autobiographical, self-reflective practice affected by changed outside realities, and how can it be responsive to such changes? Since 1983, Jo Spence and I had been evolving and developing a new photographic practice – phototherapy. Linking the discourses of representation and the notions of conscious and unconscious identities, we added therapeutic skills to the creation of images, taking turns to be sitter/director and phototherapist. All this work is about process, change and transformations. Bringing theories, issues, ideas and intuition to exploring personal stories,

**Who's guilty? In re-enacting my
father's anger, I find my own.**
In collaboration with Jo Spence

Dapper Daddy.
In collaboration with Jo Spence

through re-enacting tiny details and fragments of memories, has
enabled me to unpick the complex web of distress, pain and trauma
from my past. Working with Jo Spence enabled me to make visible
aspects long repressed or denied, and to get behind the screen
memories, the simplifications and myths of others, to at last tell my
own stories from my point of view. I also took up the positions of
my mother and father, both in relation to myself as a child, and to
explore their own histories. I found, on reflection, that I was also
exploring aspects of my own psychic reality, which I had absorbed
from and projected on to them.

A sudden disjunction. I was catapulted into new realities by events
outside my control.

In-dependence day?
Extracts from my diary:
> *4 July 1990*
> I have been with my father for weeks now, spending my days
> at the hospital, as he struggles and rasps through either the
> nebuliser or oxygen mask to keep breathing. Inhale, exhale,
> inhale, exhale. His hands held tight in fists, all his willpower

Felixstowe, 1926.

Archive of

Mrs Olive Martin

Felixstowe, August 1927.

Archive of Mrs Olive Martin

In the back garden, 1947.

Archive of Mrs Olive Martin

and energy focused down, day and night, to holding on to life. Inhale, exhale, inhale, exhale. Sometimes his anger explodes. 'You are trying to kill me, get me out of here. Take me home, 50 Ravensbury Avenue, Morden, Surrey. If you are my daughter, take me home.' Inhale, exhale, inhale, exhale. Sometimes he looks up, doe-like pleading eyes, 'I am no use to anyone any more. I cannot fight for myself.' So I try to protect him, fight for his rights. Inhale, exhale, inhale, exhale.

Sometimes I sit, concentrating on breathing in time with him. Inhale, exhale, inhale, exhale. A meditation of wills. Inhale, exhale, inhale, exhale. I massage his brow, his feet. Gently, now, relax. Inhale, exhale, inhale, exhale. The hospital routine continues, contextualising panic, powerlessness, this state of not knowing. Inhale, exhale, inhale, exhale. Slowly and relentlessly his body is depleted, as each breath requires more and more effort than the preceding one. Inhale, exhale, inhale, exhale. The doctors gathered round to stare at his X-rays in disbelief. How could he have lived so long with only 10 per cent lung function? Inhale, exhale, inhale, exhale.

But today is different, today there is no hope, today the doctors finally admit defeat, although they have trouble with the word death. Too late now for admission to the hospice that we had petitioned for, I demand a decent, more private place for him to die than the barren, open, 30-bed ward of peeling paint, of bustling activity. When he could still speak he'd accused us of taking him to a workhouse, that residual fear and threat from his childhood mythology.

The ward sister called me aside. 'Do you want him to have an extra dose of morphine?'

I check with her: 'Is it true that the morphine will give him the sleep that his tenacity has denied for so long? Is there a risk that he will relax so much that he will stop breathing?'

'Yes.'

'Yes.' It's his time to let go. Can I let go?

Outside at last, into this heavy late afternoon. I contemplate the sharp edge between life and death, this greatest burden of responsibility. I reach in my bag for my tobacco, and slowly roll a cigarette. I inhale deeply. I have to suppress my tears as they well up, my fears as they paralyse me, I have to hold myself together to support my mother through this, the worst time in her life. In sharp relief, as my father lies dying in the respiratory ward, I inhale the self-same poison. I must separate from these dependencies.

Today this process begins...

5 July 1990
My mother and I go back to hospital, this one last time. We
must sign for his things, now in a grey polythene bag marked
'NHS patient's property'. I ask to see him. At first my mother
is unsure; I know I must.

   Again we walk through seemingly endless corridors, she
so slowly, in so much pain from her arthritis. Time is
suspended. They have laid him out in the chapel of rest. He
looks so handsome, like an archetype of the wise old man,
the venerable elder. I reach out to touch him, to stroke his
brow just one more time. I register the shock of cold flesh, of
familiarity. I lift the shroud to check his hands. The right is
still fisted, tenaciously stubborn; the left has relaxed, opened,
accepting death? Soft, warm tears flow, uncheckable. I step
back so my mother may begin her goodbyes to 65 years of
knowing and being with him. As we left she said, 'Do close
the door properly, dust is so bad for him, for his chest.' Not
any more, I think.

Although I had my camera with me, I could barely allow myself to
take photographs of his decline, out of respect for him. The images,
however, remain with me, the pathos of his impotent anger, unable
to affect decisions, or the final outcome. With the finality of death, I
did take up my camera again, to create an alternative diary/family
album. Death is a taboo subject in late 20th-century western
culture, now almost bereft of ritual. I needed to use photography to
help me deal with this crisis, and my ongoing bereavement process.
I had to mark this loss for myself.

   So I photographed. I needed a record; a fixing in time of this
period of intense grief. I needed, too, I find on reflection, some of
the distance and objectivity that the act of photographing provides
to ward off the feelings of being overwhelmed, of over-
identification and of despair. I photographed through my tears and
created for myself a document of loss. This, then, was no denial,
rather a confrontation with death, with bereavement, that allowed
me, slowly, to come to terms with mortality, both his and my own.

   I laid out his belongings, collected from the hospital, that stood
in for all those hours of patient hoping and waiting, and
photographed. I took the responsibility for dealing with all the
administrative work that surrounds death, which I documented. I
discovered some anomalies; I was forbidden to photograph the
open death register showing his entry, in contrast to that stock-in-
trade image used by high-street photographers of couples signing
the marriage register.

   I recognise the significance of ritual, and the importance of

**Memento mori manifest,
July 1990.**

Rosy Martin

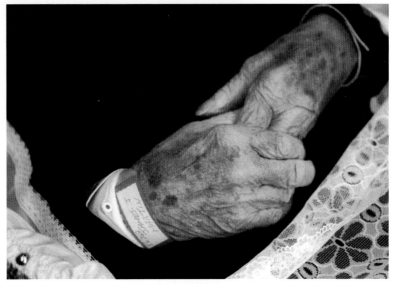

making our own rituals to mark times of transition when those that
pre-exist are institutionalised or feel out of our control. Intuitively I
knew I had to create my own ritual of reparation, separation and
grief. I collected together objects that symbolised aspects of him
and his life: a needle for his trade as a tailor and designer, a
paintbrush for his skills as an artist, a ruler for his ability to make
and invent things and his perfectionism, a sprig of rosemary, a
traditional symbol of remembrance and my given name. In his
garden I cut a rose from each bush, a spray of London Pride and

honesty and leaves from every tree and shrub. I collected old family album photographs and the photography work which I had already done about him and my relationship to him.

I asked my mother, in exchange for taking all the practical responsibilities, for one hour with 'my father', or rather his corpse, at the undertaker's. I placed, one by one, the objects I had selected into his hand or on to his body, and photographed. Whilst I worked I talked with him – strange how the newly dead seem almost to answer – honouring my memories of him in all his aspects, accepting too the angry, frustrated, bitter and difficult man that he also was. Then I put the needle in the back of his lapel, where he always kept one, the photographs in his inside breast pocket, the ruler and paintbrush in the other, and the leaves and flowers in a bouquet in his hand. I invited my mother to join me. 'You've made him look so lovely,' she said.

How anxiously I took these rolls of film to the developer's, knowing they were unrepeatable – my subject now was only ashes. It has been said that in experiencing the death of a parent the individual comes face to face with his or her own mortality.

Being in my parents' house, the home I had grown up in, now seemed strangely ghostly. Sometimes he'd called it the 'millstone around my neck', this house for which they had mortgaged themselves to the hilt 60 years before, when their landlord threatened eviction and they had a tiny baby. Now everything I looked at or touched brought him back. He had done all the decorating, creating a Tudor dining room, a Georgian parlour, a formica Fifties kitchen; he had made the furniture, the curtains, the upholstery, his water-colour and oil paintings decorated every wall; his traces were everywhere. I photographed the house, from my point of view as a child: his clothes, his empty chair, his things and his private space – the shed at the bottom of the garden.

Absent father

Early morning Sunday sunrise. Daddy says: 'Do you want to come for a drive to Box Hill?'

'Yes, yes.' I sit as upright as I can on the soft blue leather seat that sticks to my knickers, my eyes on stilts. I pull myself up to look out of the window, big girl in the front seat. Ah, Box Hill. 'Funny name for a place,' I say.

'It's because of the box trees, they grow wild and huge here,' he says. We get out. I look up, up and obediently hold his hand, although really I'd rather run off and explore. It's special to be here, today, just me and Daddy. We walk together under the huge trees. He points out the intertwining patterns in the bark, the roots, growing deep into the

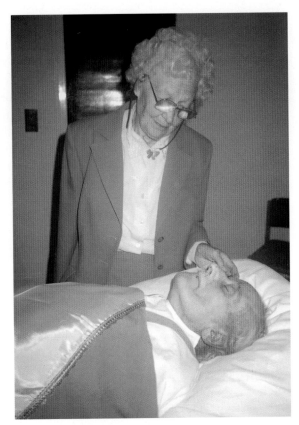

The 'site' of death, July 1990.

Rosy Martin

Last goodbye, July 1990.

Rosy Martin

hillside, and how the beech trees have grown, bracing themselves to withstand the wind, to reach for the light. 'When I die, I want my ashes scattered here, so I can gaze out over the valley. No dark cemetery of brooding yew for me,' he says. I'm not thinking of endings, only of now, as I scamper through the leaves, look up and smile back at him.

I kept my promise. Together with Mum I find a fine, tall beech tree, golden in the September sun. I take the urn, and slowly, carefully scatter the ashes in the hollow between the roots. 'Don't just leave him there, so exposed,' she says. So we cover the ashes with dead leaves. I look down. My hands are stained white with absence.

Are you wondering what my mother thought about these photographs? She was so pleased to have these last images of him, this final look. Photographs cannot heal the pain of bereavement, but they do offer a trigger to memories. I have always been concerned in my practice with challenging taboos and representing the unrepresentable. These photographs offer a means of thinking through feelings, feeling through thoughts.

Dedications
I dedicate this piece to the memory of James John Martin, my father, in loving respect and acceptance that he did the best he could, within the limitations that he perceived.
I dedicate this piece to the memory of Jo Spence, in memory of all the fun, work and insights we shared.
I would also like to thank Eve Cunningham and Cora Greenhill, for sharing their integration of new rituals into everyday life. This helped me to intuitively create my own rituals when I needed to.

brenda prince

a letter to my mother

Photo: Maggie Murray

Dear Mum,

It was good to see you this weekend in your new home. I always
come away from you feeling slightly depressed and guilty. Guilty
for not being the daughter you would have liked me to have
been. I know you would have liked me to have settled down and

married, had kids – grandchildren – and lived in a nice house, probably not far from you. I know you're disappointed. I've always felt this and feel that I've let you down.

I've never been a conventional daughter. I remember in my teens slouching around in jeans and shirts; not wearing 'feminine' clothes, not wearing make-up. 'How do you expect to attract boys?' you would ask. I know you both referred to me as a tomboy and hoped I would grow out of it. I also remember how I screwed up my courage years later, after three days and sleepless nights worrying about how you would react to my telling you I was gay, and how we both burst into tears when I did. But you didn't throw me out or reject me. I think you just hoped it would go away.

I knew you were upset, though, and remember Dad, weeks later, speaking for both you, asking: 'You don't expect us to be proud of you, do you? To me you're just a freak of nature.' I got upset and very angry and told you that I wasn't prepared to put my head in a gas oven and that unless you accepted me for what I was, I wouldn't come home any more. (Remember, I'd just started living and working in London at that time.) I left. Months later you wrote to me and apologised on behalf of Dad. He just had a bad way of expressing himself. The ice was broken and we resumed a tentative relationship. Now, 16 years later, you're telling me you have bought a new bed to put in the spare room for when my partner and I come to stay!

I know you saw me as a difficult child and I even felt you loved William more than me because he was a more easy-going and sensitive child than I was. But I'm glad I was difficult and stroppy or I would never have had the courage to accept my lesbianism. And I do wholeheartedly. I've never been happier since the day I 'came out' – to myself and to my friends. I know you will never understand my loving women, Mum. I wish you could. As a baby you were the first person I loved and despite what Freud said was supposed to happen... well, it didn't. I'm not a pervert. I'm just different. I was born a lesbian and I'm glad of it.

Do you remember when I left home to live in London? As the train passed by our back garden you waved a white sheet out of a bedroom window in farewell, as I hadn't wanted you to see me off at the station. I knew it would be too painful. I cried my eyes out and had to hide behind a newspaper so that no one would see me. I loved you then, Mum, and still do (and Dad too).

    Hugs and everything
    Brenda.

This small piece is dedicated to Jo Spence, who encouraged me to take a degree at PCL and who also had trouble in conforming.

discovering new directions

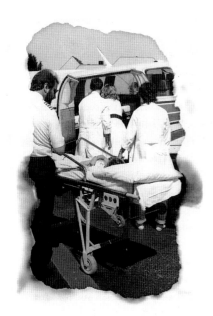

Until recently, using the camera represented a problematic area for me inasmuch as I found it difficult to justify a disjointed accumulation of isolated moments. Trapped memories with little context. Launching out on to a fine art degree three years ago helped me towards visualising ways in which photos could be selectively used, not just to represent different aspects of my life but also, more broadly, as a starting point for discussion. In other words, to use my camera as an enabling tool. By making visible unseen aspects of our lives, not only are we helped to come to terms with them ourselves, but we can realise and represent them as being valuable rather than insignificant.

Like so many others, I have in the past used my camera on holidays to create a total illusion of scenic views and happy faces. That was until a holiday in 1988 when my youngest daughter suffered a traumatic accident and needed major surgery. While I was with her 24 hours a day for eight days, my sense of time distorted and disrupted, the camera was an aid to coping with the situation. Through the lens I could both be subjectively intuitive and feel objectively in control in powerless circumstances. I ultimately compiled this material with careful consideration to present to others in a very personal book.

However, perhaps it is important to have not only particular incidents which break through the confines of the traditional subject matter of snapshots included in the family album, but also manifestations of a general way of life and its changes. Spending the last four years as a mature student has introduced me to exciting new horizons. It has helped me to unlock many things within myself, but it has also brought its share of dilemmas and conflicts. Discovering new directions and potentials, having the chance to grow and develop, precipitates a reassessment of your entire sense of identity and questions your role within the family.

The problem is how to maintain the balance between both mother/wife and this new sense of womanhood without making it oppositional.

Working on photographs for the family album allows me to take a critical look at my position. It also puts me in a situation where I can see myself learning to find my feet and to articulate. It gives me the opportunity to send out clues as to where I am and what I am thinking.

In this piece of work I use the table as a motif – the one place where a family sits down together. But is this 'togetherness' merely an ideal we feel we have to live up to?

opposite

The image of this poor, shrivelled up, strung up chicken struck me as important largely because it refers back to an earlier piece of work I did in black and white. In this montage tableau I re-enacted a kitchen scene from a Dutch painting, repositioning it in a contemporary setting in order to examine the role of women in the kitchen, as well as the representation of women. I did this by placing a woman on the table posed in the shape of a chicken. Another woman stands behind with knives ready to carve up. Woman as a hunk of meat, as a consumable item. So seeing this frazzled chicken waiting for my family to cut it up and eat it became an extension of that other work. This, for me, expresses strong needs for, and dependency upon, each other, whilst we simultaneously 'feed' off each other. With the original 'chicken' piece existing more firmly in an art rather than a family album context, it is important for me to be able to make references to it within my family album to link my home and my art work.

Getting my daughter to take a photo of me washing the floor from above expressed my point of view quite clearly. But it was equally intended as a comment on the nature of housework – its belittling nature and its invisibility. The collapsing washing line is an attempt at a positive demonstration of the interdependence of apparently separate issues. The line is collapsing in spite of (as well as because of) me, but I am determinedly stopping its total collapse, although at the same time becoming enmeshed and entangled in its web.

My increasing involvement and commitment over the last four years as a visual artist has created a shift, a dilemma. Whereas originally housework was more a question of logistics, of physically managing to do justice to home and degree course, as my own self-awareness and self-expectations grew it developed into more complex, abstract areas of identity, role conflict and dependence. It grew from being not only my point of view but one involving others' conceptions and misconceptions of the situation as well.

In selecting photos for my family album which try to make visual the inside working of my family rather than give an idealised version of it, I am aware of their catalytic potential. Although it might be said that by exposing fears and tensions you encourage openness and discussion, there is still a danger that the very process of visualisation will demand a fair amount of readjustment by all concerned.

It's always a matter of trying to find that fine balance.

The final photo of my desk is a representation of me. My desk is a very special place for me, somewhere I spend a lot of my time. It is my sanctuary amidst books and ideas which stimulate and inspire me and it is a sanctuary situated deep within my family, whom I need for their love and support.

psychic manure and political issues

woman in secret

'SECRET: *hidden, concealed, secluded, unseen, unknown, private, recondite, latent, covert, clandestine, privy.*'
Webster's Synonyms, Antonyms and Homonyms

**The inner shame
of our ugliness.**

There are many kinds of secrets. Public secrets, private secrets. Malevolent secrets, benign secrets. Shameful secrets, profitable secrets. There are professional or religious secrets involving protocols, doctrines and ceremonies which are kept from the uninitiated, dividing 'them' from 'us'. Some secrets are censored from public scrutiny by ministerial decree for national security and political expediency. Whole groups of people, institutions, companies or bureaucracies share in (and depend upon the keeping of) secrets to maintain their power. There are also secrets we have been encouraged to collude in, including economic and political crimes. Secrets form the media's staple diet of the intimacies of the rich, the royal and the famous, exhorting us to gorge upon them.

Then there are just plain, old-fashioned, family secrets. Some we are unlucky enough to inherit from others, like skeletons under floorboards; others are hidden from us in an attempt to protect us until later when we move into the wider world. Only then do we learn that society has little value for our particular type or group, with all the ensuing denial of our roots. Others involve things done to us of which we are too frightened to speak (or which, if we dared, have been dismissed as lies or fantasies). Most pernicious are those which become entwined with our innermost terrors of perceived inadequacies in a thousand shades of impotence, disability or ugliness. Joyfully, there are those which we initiate, like being gay, or having a special place no one knows about, planning surprises, or loving or hating someone we aren't supposed to. Sometimes one family member and not others are in the know. For 30 years a friend never knew her father had committed suicide;

**Public secrets,
private secrets...**

**My brother was born
'unexpectedly' when
I was four.**

another was not told she had a Jamaican grandfather.

Working life is saturated with secrets. So is the exchange of money. Once when I worked as a book-keeper on the wages at a large farm I was literally sworn to secrecy not to divulge one person's earnings to another as each job had been negotiated separately. Most secrets shake off their potency with time as social mores or alliances change, but others never lose their ability to traumatise us if we fear that we are in danger of being 'found out'. Societies seem to thrive and survive on secrets.

From the jumble of secrets I once held, I now couldn't care less who knows that I use an inhaler for my asthma, or that both my parents worked in factories, or that I was a petty thief, or (what I hid from my parents for years) that I 'lived in sin' as a young woman, later perversely getting married in secret. Nor does it any longer matter that for years I was in love with Dirk Bogarde only to be shattered by his secret (his homosexuality), hating my male rivals clamouring alongside me at the stage door. Worse still, that I once joined the Liberal party, or called the sitting room the lounge! But I still quake at the thought of being seen in public without my dentures. Conversely, I am pleased to collude in being told that I don't 'look my age', but not to publicise that I am celibate and post-menopausal. In terms of public secrets I make no bones about having cancer (unlike millions of others who are whispered about), which has empowered me to run the gauntlet of the medical orthodoxy, using my camera to campaign against their inadequacies. Of course, for a secret to no longer exist, there are as many different investments in revelation as there are in making and keeping it in the first place.

The widespread uses of photography, both in the professional and popular spheres, whilst appearing to democratise and offer the potential to reveal all secrets and tell us 'the truth', in reality can't really do any such thing and many compound and conceal the real secrets. For a start there are no simple truths, only fragmentary and multiple perceptions seen through the structures of our (and others') fantasies, which then have to be made sense of in the light of other knowledge. A first step towards this for me was to learn how changing the text of a picture could entirely alter its meanings. Never is this clearer than when I'm looking through my family albums as I've added different layers of meaning across the years. I now see my pictures at most as clues or traces, at least as screens on to which I can project my own fantasies, or as shielding me from countless events and secrets. As family historian I could shout with frustration at how little I still understand even now about my own past. I wish my mother had been able to use a camera so that I could begin to speculate more as to what kind of person she was in the period before she gave birth to me.

A landfill site in Nottingham. Every year millions of tons of personal and familial ephemera are trashed. We need to pay more attention to such artifacts and begin to develop historical imagination.

I still have to admit, though, I do love secrets. Especially other people's! Until recently, most of my own, and those of my family, were kept under wraps out of mistaken and tangled notions of family loyalty, fear and shame. A prime example of this was my mother's euthanasia. My brother and I were afraid to even whisper about how we were involved in her medically provoked death. Instead, across the years a vast and prolonged silence ensued. Even the idea of taking a photograph of her dead or dying, in order perhaps to be able to discuss her in the future and to mourn her properly, would have filled me with horror. Instead I cut myself off from my feelings and 'forgot about it'. Only now, 17 years later, with the doctor who collaborated dead and thus beyond prosecution, has it been possible to face the spectre and to talk about it with my brother. But it is still painful to feel it. Perhaps death is still the biggest secret? Very often we are forced to keep injustices or injuries done to us and to others a secret, rendering ourselves speechless out of shame, terror or fear of stigmatisation, thus often perpetuating the situation. Speaking out might help change things but it might also get us into a whole lot of trouble – there can be no 'armies of one'. We need to be sure we have support before taking the plunge, as in the case of incest survival, wife- or child-battering, or in sexual, racial, class or age harassment. Going public by speaking or showing our pictures as evidence can sometimes encourage others to join in and shift the balance of power or opinion, as is often apparent when issues become politicised. Less globally, getting a sibling or colleague to hear our side of the story and to become our 'advocate' might make us feel stronger in facing up to a bully. But, whilst self-silencing might help us to at least keep going, it means our emotions are never quite straightforward as we learn to filter out our feelings of anger or powerlessness, and often it leads to depression. So where does all that repressed anger go? One of my first steps towards letting go of depression was to learn assertiveness training. I also learned for the first time to keep a diary (ranting on paper) as one way to vent a range of emotions and pleasures. I also trained myself to keep visual diaries and a creative journal [1] for similar reasons.

This still didn't seem enough to give expression to the bottomless pit of my emotions and so I moved beyond photography, learning some of the skills of art therapy in order to discover the secrets of my own dreams and subconscious thoughts. But although I have begun to keep very detailed documents I still can't quite mark out my deepest thoughts or secrets. I still have the feeling that somebody is looking over my shoulder; that he or she will judge or abandon me. David, my husband, who works as a systems analyst, has no such problems. Sitting right under my nose, he taps away in code into his tiny microwriter before storing his thoughts on disks with fancy names. At one point he shared a few pages of his erotic fantasies as kept in dream diaries, which he buries somewhere in the attic, and we felt very close as we giggled together. Then he clammed up again, climbed the ladder back into the roof with them, and I've not heard a whisper since.

By the age of 15, with my first simple Box Brownie, I had begun to document my own life. Having my own camera seemed to allow me access to forbidden places, giving me a fleeting sense of power. But I can see now that what I thought of then as 'my life' existed mostly in the few surviving snapshots of either joky or highly idealised scenarios. For some inexplicable reason I also seem to have photographed flowers a lot! Although I love my pictorial scraps, when I look at what is left I find nothing much of any significance and would love at least to have some traces of everyday life. Of course, I do have memories which go beyond my snapshots and in the early days family secrets ranged from the profound, such as the sudden arrival of a baby brother, to the trivial, hiding toothache from my mother for fear of the dentist. Later there were also incomprehensible secrets. For instance, my belief that my father had lost his mother as a young lad was shattered, along with my faith that he never lied, after my teenage brother came home from a spiritualist seance and announced that heaven was rubbish because he'd 'got a message from my grandmother who had just "passed over"'. As we didn't have any grandmothers this seemed positive proof of spiritual fraud. I'll never forget my father's face amidst our laughter as he heard this. Next day at supper Dad announced that he felt it was time to tell us that his mother had not (as legend had it) died when a bomb hit the house in the first world war. Instead she had lost her mind and been locked up in an asylum and had died there peacefully a few days before. Only in retrospect

left **In my early scrapbooks I looked at contradictions.**

right **Now I plunge into the secrets I've always hidden from myself and begin to deal with them.**

did I understand the stigma attached to her 'madness' and also begin to comprehend my grandfather's strange behaviour with his live-in 'housekeeper', who also worked in the ironmongery corner shop of the terrace of houses in which they lived. Neither grandmother nor housekeeper appeared anywhere in the family album and it was as if my grandfather had immaculately conceived six children. How did this secret, this hole, this structured absence in our history, warp my father's life and our later ability to be open with each other as a family?

Growing out of my early post-war meanderings as teenager-with-camera, my love of unravelling secrets is probably why I chose to become a professional portrait photographer in the 1960s. Since early childhood evacuations in wartime I had always felt myself to be an outsider. It seemed that if I couldn't join in then I could at least become a sanctioned voyeur. I'd also learned the exquisite joys of keeping my own secrets, particularly from my parents. Part of the power and pleasure of some secrets is that some of us are in the know and not others. My most potent weaponry with which to

Going back to the site of my early sexual graveyard encounters with my camera taught me a lot about myself.

upset their 'respectability' was stealing. This was never haphazard but always planned. Not only for the joy of getting the coveted object or the needed money to squander on schoolfriends, but also for the ritual of defiance. Luckily I never got caught. Later, when my sexuality blossomed in dark alleyways and cemeteries, I intuited that my mother was 'not interested' in my innocent explorations and I learned yet again to keep my mouth closed (and my legs open). In those days most of my secret life was to do with the opposite sex. Yet memory plays tricks as one pattern clangs against another, for even if my deepest secret was how ugly and unlovable I was I still seem to have attracted a lot of attention – mostly from boys of whom my parents did not approve. My photos of this period contain only the usual bland expressions of my 'good' behaviour.

On a recent research trip to one of the large colour film-processing factories I watched endless ribbons of prints coming off the production line. Amongst the sunsets, military parades, weddings and holidays were thousands of pictures of people in various states of undress: where do people put these images? I have never found any in a single shoebox or family album I have looked at. Clearly people take a much wider range of pictures than we ever see or talk about.

Although I come from a 'happy family', how I longed at the same time for a family where I was listened to, and where my sexuality could have been open and joyful instead of passively rebellious and covert. Recently I went back to the cemetery and took pictures of the sites of my repressed desires. I learned a lot about myself from that visit.

In relation to the innermost sanctum of my secrets, the most painful of all is to do with class codes of conduct, of which I

I re-enact my mother's 'crime' (secret) of being a factory worker and double-shift mother.

below

Re-enacting (with Rosy Martin) my cross-dressing as a child/adult in 1949.

became aware by the age of six when, as an evacuee, I moved rapidly between people of different class factions and was continually exhorted to behave and speak in a variety of ways. This continued into my formal schooling. There is no acknowledgement of the painful self-censorship or secrecy involved in such acts of domination and subordination when I look at the pictures of this period, nor is it ever openly talked about. By my teens I was caught up in a complex range of class and sexual masquerades which now extended beyond language and behaviour and began to take the form of 'personal style'. As a child longing to be an adult, each day, at the moment of freedom from school as I passed through the gates, I could transform my clothing into something alluring with the merest undoing of a couple of buttons and the removal of my filthy ankle socks. Recently I re-enacted my fantasy of the confusion of this cross-dressing and was astonished to see the obviousness of what I'd thought so pleasurably subtle at the time.

By the time I started work as a typist I was involved in 'triple talk'. I talked posh at work – friends never recognised the voice answering the telephone as mine.

Here I was taught to be outwardly obedient, tidy and to dress tastefully. In my free time I soon reverted to my streetwise, sexualised, tomboy self, transforming back into 'good virgin daughter' at home. These rapid shifts of identity and language were compounded by my place in the class pecking order as I learned to be attractive to young men from middle-class homes, learned different class manners and witnessed their belief system in operation. How I longed to be like them. Yet I always felt inadequate in ways I could never articulate or share. Nor could I easily assimilate as I felt my lack of formal education and 'good breeding' contributed to my feelings of not belonging. Under the surface there was always a latent terror at being found wanting. Criss-crossing class boundaries involves a complexity of choices of naming or not naming, of renaming and half naming when in 'mixed company'. As I grew more daring I began to lose sight of who I was within my inner core in the informally choreographed

A typical snapshot of me from my teens as I try to conceal, yet again, my class origins.

In 1979 I enrol as a mature student and for three years hide my terror of being 'found out' under a welter of obsessive study and paper writing.

dance of 'thems' and 'mes'. Later, in my mid-forties, as a mature student I re-experienced all these terrors as I worked unnecessarily hard to get my degree, moving now between different kinds of everyday and theoretical languages.

Nowadays I feel less vulnerable and dig up my psychic manure and spread it around with relish. In my work as a social historian and phototherapist I now see that some secrets can be confused with social taboos; imposed upon us rather than instigated by us. I now use my snapshot camera whenever I feel I can detect something important in my own life which I want to resist remembering. Even the tiniest visual clues have helped me. I've also begun to take sporadic snapshots out on the streets, where I record tiny signs of the changing face of everyday life as Britain continues to move into a deeper economic crisis. Here I am constantly struck by the contradiction of the widespread publication (for a range of reasons) of what, to the people referred to in the images, are often the deepest of private secrets.

I have also begun to use my studio camera to re-enact repressed memories and fantasies of the past, making 'part self' portraits of myself or my mother with the help of colleagues Terry Dennett and Rosy Martin. [2] The meanings of these shift all the time as new combinations and montages of pictures emerge, and I have also begun to be aware of how differently the same events can be perceived. Building on work evolved with Terry on what we called the 'theatre of the self', Rosy and I started to use techniques learned from being in therapy. We found great safety in working together to make pictures because many aspects of our class histories overlapped and it felt safe to speak – and to show things – freely to each other. Using the camera in all these different ways has been for me like searching for clues and making them visible as bits of unsolved mysteries. This was the most profound of all the work I'd done on myself, for once I began to recognise the secrets which I was hiding from myself, then I could set about finding ways of changing things. But this was never easy as, like all humans, I have a compulsion to repeat things in the familiar (if unworkable) ways I've always followed. Sometimes I don't even know why I have taken a photograph, but later I usually see how it 'fits in'. If my conscious eye is sleeping or afraid, my guardian eye often reminds me to take pictures. It was only in recent years in the safety of therapy that I found myself able to inhabit again these earlier selves, with all the loathing for self alongside the envy I had felt for others. As I hit rock bottom and the complex masquerade fell to pieces through mental and physical breakdown I saw that my illness was trying to speak to me and to give me a legitimate opportunity to be reclusive and to spend time relearning about myself.

Some of my snapshots of everyday street life. Some secrets become too huge to remain secret. Yet we, as individuals to whom such things 'just happen', very often keep them secret from our nearest and dearest.

In my public work on secrets and taboos I have often chosen to highlight aspects of my life because I want to share insights and political concerns and to get feedback by going public. Sometimes the biggest secrets of all are right out there in the open but we can't recognise them for what they are. I've had a lot of flak for my work on the mistaken assumption that it is some kind of narcissism rather than politically motivated investigation. Using the camera in these ways has shown me that I have no fixed identity and that my subjectivity is always in process rather than a 'positive' or 'negative' thing to be spoken about from outside. Critical academics have found it difficult to comprehend an endeavour to find a 'subject language' when they are so highly trained as professional managers of knowledge, deeply implicated in concealing their own feelings and class histories. I've also had positive feedback from people all over the world, encouraging me to go on making it safe for others to dig into their histories, repressed feelings and fantasies. I see my artworks as a kind of 'politicised exhibitionism' about particular psychic and social issues which have enraged me. In this respect I have used myself as

**Our secret
selves. David and
I are so open with
each other it is
the joy of my life.**

a kind of case study. Overall, though, most of the work I have done is only for myself and will always be very private as I consider it of no relevance to others.

These days I don't have many secrets from myself, but I still choose to keep some from other people. The point of all the unravelling was to try to understand the past in order to have some peace in the present and move into the future in the light of new knowledge. Free of bogies which have been transformed, and as someone with a life-threatening illness, I think now that most important of all is to find the secret of my malfunctioning blood and liver. I can't imagine that taking snapshots will be of much use to me here, though, except to mark out the peaks and troughs of my journey with David through illness and potential recovery. Soon there will come a time when I cease to analyse and probe altogether and take up some 'hobbies'. I have already begun gardening, thus seeming to have gone full circle by starting to photograph flowers again!

I feel there is good reason for each of us to consider using our cameras more thinkingly, rather than slavishly. Constructing our

Me with some of
my 'part-selves'.

own meanings of the world out of the complexity of who we think
we are, of what we think the world is. Looking at the whole range
of secrets from those of the state right through to those which we
know about but hide from ourselves. Such personal activity is not
to replace the question of political action because that is also
needed, but to see how acting as individuals and as groups is
interconnected. Perhaps we can also begin to develop the idea of an
historical imagination so that we leave behind us documents and
archives for others to inherit which are more than a few bits of
paper and anecdotes about family life.

1. See especially Ira Progoff, *At a Journal Workshop.*
2. Working with Rosy Martin and Terry Dennett has been referred to in detail
in my book *Putting Myself in the Picture,* Camden Press, 1986.

politics in perspective

Some years ago my son and his girlfriend bought me my first camera as a Christmas present. Although I couldn't afford to buy many films and get them developed and printed I still enjoyed taking pictures, mostly of my garden and in the local park. I used to wait for the squirrels to come down out of the trees and I especially enjoyed photographing the sunsets. As my son is a photographer he always encouraged me. Before I got a camera I relied on family and friends to take photographs, mostly of visits out to see the family and on the odd holiday that our son or daughter took us on. I ended up with an odd assortment of pictures of my grandchildren which don't mean very much now as I never wrote dates or details on the backs. I really regret that I didn't take more trouble over keeping our family's history.

When I think back on my life now, hardly anything was ever photographed. For example, my earliest memory of my father is when he returned home after four years in the trenches in the first world war. He was caked in mud, so much so that the only way to remove his clothes was to cut them off with a pair of scissors. The second world war corresponded with the beginning of my young married life. Everybody I knew worked for long hours in munitions as well as running a home and looking after a family, queuing up for things like whale meat (which was a treat). Needless to say, none of this was photographed, much less the bombing which went on for days on end. When I came to read about the war years later I discovered that so few photographs were taken because the government had made it illegal for people to take pictures of the damage and the deaths. My grandchildren can hardly believe any of this when I tell them now. I also have very few pictures of my mother and father. There is one of my father, who was a master plasterer and worked till the age of 76. He's sitting in a studio in front of a fake balustrade on a posh chair in his best suit. He looks

Coming from a family which taught me self-reliance is specially useful now that I'm a pensioner. It's ironic to think that I am in the same position now as my parents were all those years ago, with no more money or possessions and hardly any real social change. Of course, our back garden's not big enough to keep a pig but we do have a good assortment of local charity shops where we can rummage for clothes. This might seem a strange thing to photograph but I am really keen that my family understand what our life is like now.

very dignified and proud; not a bit how I remember him when he got home each night from work covered in white powder. None of the few pictures which have survived show the interesting and self-reliant life which they led. They used to keep chickens and a pig in the back garden and my mother used to make bread and potato and dandelion wines and prepare all our medicines using herbs.

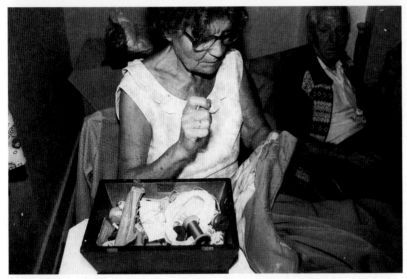

There is a tradition in many working-class families of staying out of the hands of state and welfare officials. This means very often having to do things for ourselves which we could apply to have others do. We could humiliate ourselves to get a few bob more from the government, but in the end we prefer it the way we've chosen. One of the ways we've managed to make ends meet is by never throwing anything away until it's fallen to bits (and even then we can often think of something to do with the good bits!).

One luxury we do have is the telephone, plus stamp money for sending letters and photographs. They are an essential way of keeping in touch with our family.

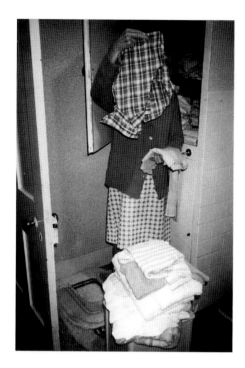

All this talk about equality for women makes me laugh. Equality with who? I sat down one evening and worked out that I had been washing towels twice a week for 55 years. I worked out that this adds up to a total of 5,280 towels. When I worked in a laundry in Essex we were washing sheets all day. I've no idea how many we washed between us but this is the only picture of me at work which I have.

Rituals

Listening to the Queen in the hope she'll say something which might be meaningful to us pensioners. I asked my son to take this picture.

A new ritual: since the 1980s I've been giving vent to my feelings about our second 'lady'. This is my 1989 contribution.

tb/aids diary

My approach to documentary photography was changing. I was questioning its effectiveness in dealing with social issues. I looked to many sources, including the images from Minatama by W. Eugene and Alleen Smith and photographs of illness by the English photographer Jo Spence. These photographs seemed religious and political, yet accessible and structurally powerful. I attended the Breadloaf Writers' Conference and studied with author Francine Prose, who spoke about creating dialogue in which 'you see into a person's heart'. I read the

collective work of St Teresa of Avila, in which catharsis through prayer and journal writing changed her, and she became more sympathetic to suffering.

My mother's experience of stigma was to do with having TB in the 1930s and this was, for me, a starting place for new work. I constructed an image that focused directly on stigma, which I titled *Infected With*, using a matrix image of a female model that served as a mythic representation of my mother when she had TB at 20. I arranged objects: texts, media clips and my father's funeral roses. Relatives advised him not to marry my mother because she was a 'weak' woman, but he did not leave her. He was also advised not to have children, but he took that risk with her, too. Growing up with them, I saw the negative effects of stigma. My father had earned a Purple Heart after being wounded in the second world war, but as a returned disabled army veteran, at 36 he was unable to walk without pain, or to work full-time again. He was periodically told he had a year left to live. His funeral roses, when fresh, evoked the beauty and caring in my father; withered, they represented the stigma and the prophecy of an early death. The pain and otherness in his life were conditions which I knew that people with AIDS would experience too.

With *TB/AIDS Diary* I wanted to address the issue of stigma surrounding contagious disease by comparing my mother's stigma in having tuberculosis in the 1930s to the stigma surrounding AIDS sufferers today. In 1986, when I began using TB as a metaphor for stigma, it had been almost eradicated. A few months later, the American Lung Association announced it as a disease of AIDS and that it was spreading again. To my horror both the diseases continue to plague the world. My *TB/AIDS Diary* evolved in that year when galleries asked me to donate photographs for AIDS fund-raising auctions. I had heard in the news that people with AIDS were having trouble finding housing and were being ostracised in the workplace. I remembered, from seeing the diary that my mother kept in the TB sanatorium, that people were afraid to have former TB patients over to dinner; employers often didn't hire them back after recovery and lovers didn't wait for the completion of the one- to two-year cures.

Photo-Metro magazine published the TB diary and shortly afterwards I met author Eric Marcus, who suggested that I make the connection between TB and AIDS more explicit. AIDS continued to escalate and I felt I wanted to make a stronger statement. He put me in touch with Barbara Cleaver, whose son Scott died of AIDS in the 1980s. She herself is founder of a mothers of AIDS patients group. At that time little was known about AIDS.

After corresponding with her, I received her speeches and snapshots. The night of their arrival I had a dream and wrote in my

journal: 'I am stained. Dried blood, mud, my pen, the stain does not wash out. It is on the surface of my skin. It pervades my body – all the flesh and bone.' The psychic weight hovering around AIDS was hard for me, but I decided to make a parallel sequence of AIDS-related images using a matrix of a male model layered with snapshots of Mrs Cleaver and her son, excerpts from her letters and symbols of stigma. I had chosen the somewhat crude, hand-made, family album form for the photo collages, as I wanted the images to work together, both as poetry and documentary. I felt committed to reaching audiences, because I believe that art is a form of information. I wanted to assist in AIDS prevention, so I spent time showing 11x14 Cibacopy prints to editors of health periodicals, producers at public TV stations, gatekeepers of newsletters and non-profit spaces. As it gained coverage, photography publications and museums contacted me to get involved with AIDS. With the assistance of Polaroid, I made larger 20x24 colour Polaroid prints for them.

TB/AIDS Diary has been featured in media (including the *Philadelphia Inquirer* and *Newsday Sunday* magazines), where it is rare for collage/non-traditional documentary photography to run as a photo essay. The Rhode Island Department of Health purchased a set to circulate throughout hospitals to stimulate discussion among health personnel. After media reviews and an exhibit in Helsinki, passport stamping of HIV was stopped. It was the key exhibit/speech at the International Conference on AIDS Education, Nashville, and won the Ferguson Award from the Friends of Photography in 1989. Photography magazines *F*, (Sweden), *Creative Camera* (England), *European Photography* (Germany), among others, got involved with AIDS and presented *TB/AIDS Diary* in anticipation of the impact of epidemics. Translated into nine languages, the exhibit is travelling in museums in Portugal, Columbia, France, and the USA with over 300 articles.

TB/AIDS Diary is important because stigma around AIDS still leads to violence, hostility and isolation, promoting discrimination, not empathy. Through the exhibition one sees how Scott Cleaver and my mother relied on family love to sustain them. Many who are HIV positive or who have AIDS are not near families and are without any supportive major relationship. A government cannot give the unconditional love that normally comes from family and friends and, collectively, we still have not been capable of providing this. In one of the photo collages I asked: 'Who is not unclean?' The more of us who recognise our common bond and erase stigma for people with the disease, the better the quality of life for all.

The cultural momentum and deaths around AIDS propel my vocal activism. Two years ago, the *New York Times* and *Daily News* released the shocking news that the incidence of TB was up,

due mostly to HIV immune deficiency. Prior to this publication of statistics, because of my concerns about both diseases, I had been talking to the Baltimore TB Unit, Department of Health and to the NYC TB/AIDS Unit, Department of Health about exhibiting. The government workers who wanted the show couldn't find final support from their superiors. But on the positive side Dr John F. Murray's new paper, 'Cursed Duet: HIV Infection and Tuberculosis', was delivered at a respiratory disease conference in France and there *TB/AIDS Diary* was exhibited.

The Center for Disease Control TB Unit sent their 1993 funding plan to me for review. It finally addresses TB and education, yet leaves this to social service agencies which are awarded money. I suggested that the granting funds be available to artists and makers of information, who do not fit the application requirements. Most of the art and information generated for AIDS is utilised by such agencies, which spend millions of dollars on educating us on our well-being. AIDS pointed out to me how much work is yet to be done by artists to communicate and present our ideas in this forum and any others that need our support.

Women can do quite a lot with a camera.

lisa chell

death of a cow

I tend to work intuitively, my work always being influenced by
the environment in which it is situated and the materials which
are at hand. I had been working with images of cows and female
forms for a long time and was looking for a way to move away
completely from this type of imagery. However, as I worked to
construct a mound of mud in the middle of a piece of marshy
ground, it took on the form of a cow, an abstract form which
represented, to me, the corpse of a cow. This felt very poignant as it
suggested a way of 'killing off' the image I had wanted to escape. I
surrounded the form with dried grass and set it alight, a kind of

sacrificial offering which I thought would put an end to the matter. This was not to be as the work took on a whole new meaning. I saw the flames as a life force, suggesting images of the phoenix and rebirth. A few weeks later plants and grass had begun to grow over it and eventually the entire surface was covered, making it almost indistinguishable from its surroundings.

Why did I document the piece photographically over a period of six months? I was documenting the process of growth and erosion of a piece whose meaning touched upon regeneration as well as death and was ever-changing. It showed the inseparability of life and death. I was in the middle of a paradox. I had constructed a burial mound to celebrate the end of my dealings with female forms. The work refused to die, but arose as something new. The earth is a place for burial, but it is also a source of sustenance. In the summer (the time of year when this work was built) vegetation

is at its peak. What I discovered is that the creation of images made from the natural materials found in the living body of the earth is as much a celebration of life as it is an acknowledgement of death.

Eventually the piece was reduced to a shapeless stump and finally to a memory. My alteration to the landscape had been accepted back into the earth with the minimum of disruption. There had been an intimate fusion. I had neither destroyed nor disturbed the landscape.

I have been dealing with transience. The work as I made it had vanished, but in terms of representation it has been transformed into photographs of transience.

documentary photography

Two very personal events lie behind my basic attitude to and feelings about photography. When I was 16 someone showed me a book of the 'Family of Man' exhibition. I was completely bowled over and determined to become a photographer. I have subsequently learned to challenge the view of the world which Steichen presented – liberal, humanitarian and somewhat sentimental – and even, as a feminist, to query the very title of the exhibition. But I have never lost the sense that it gave me of photography's power to convey surface information and human emotions.

Fifteen years later, by now a working photojournalist, I was beginning to wonder, like many others, whether photography was quite as innocent as I thought. Was it objective? Or did it give us hidden messages about attitudes to women, to black people, to anyone powerless or disadvantaged? Did it show us the truth?

Then my father died. I found out that for the last 25 years, unknown to me or my brother, he had had a mistress. My mother had known, my grandmother had known; in fact, it seems, everybody had known. Worse still, they assumed I had known and disapproved. It explained many things about my family, its dynamics and its relationships. It was a shock and I have never again felt that anything in the world is clear and easily understandable. I always feel that in any situation there may be one fact, one piece of information, which, if only I knew it, would change my perceptions completely.

For months afterwards I pored over our family snaps, re-examining, looking for some clue in the pictures of my mother and father together; especially searching for the one of my father and his mistress together. And there was even a shot of him with her husband. They fascinated me and they did offer up some information, but not much and not what I really wanted to know.

Like why? And why not tell us? And why not divorce? Even the basic questions which every photojournalist's captions should answer were not resolved by the family album. Who, what, why, when and how? I had to speak to people directly to get any inkling of an answer. The pictures told me only what people looked like and that they were probably friends. His mistress told me herself why everything had been hidden – or one explanation anyway: 'For the sake of the children.' I was 32 at the time and I felt a fool.

As far as I am concerned photographs have never been the same again – neither mine nor anyone else's. More interesting in some ways; more complex and open to different interpretations, but not the same. They still have the power to engage me, excite me, move me, but always with a faint reservation, a feeling there might be 'a bit more to it'. This did not hit me in a blinding flash. At the time I was more inclined to view my changing attitude towards photography as the result of political awareness or a growing sense of responsibility. Looking back, though, I feel that it was partly public, intellectual debates that changed me, but that the energy behind those insights came from my own personal experience.

Documentary photography and photojournalism set out to record our relationship to the world and each other. Though I have been a photographer for many years, I have still not worked out an exact definition of these two terms. Because my basic subject matter has been other people and their lives, my work has been exhilarating and educational in the broadest sense. I have learned much from the people and events I have photographed. I have also had to consider many aspects of being a photographer which go beyond lighting, exposing and composing a picture. Photographers who document social situations, complex political events and sensitive issues are often confronted with questions of ethics and responsibility; real dilemmas needing practical answers.

One of the basic questions is, 'What right have we to take and publish pictures of people without their permission?' Many pictures of historical and social significance have been snatched without the subject's consent – as we unconsciously underline in the terminology we use: the photographs have been 'taken'. Sometimes the photograph's value as a document or educational tool seems to outweigh any consideration of personal inconvenience or embarrassment; still less whether it is to be welcomed and used by the subject. At other times individuals become enraged and attack or sue photographers for what they consider a breach of privacy. In some countries the law upholds an individual's wish that his or her permission be required before photographs are taken. The right to depict wars, famines, distress and misery is questioned, especially as these subjects are the staple of much magazine and news photography. Often it is not the fact that a person has been photographed that offends, but the specific way the photographer has chosen to show or 'represent' him or her – for example, as unnecessarily powerless or passive. On the whole the general public lumps all photographers together as the exploitative media. The paparazzi snatching flash pictures of Princess Di and the newshounds with a foot in the door are most people's stereotypical view of the photojournalist. It is difficult for a photographer who wants to work in a responsible and sensitive way to be accepted as a trustworthy person. Maybe there is no long-term harm in this, as it has at least led far more people to criticise the media and question the old idea that photographs tell an objective all-time truth. More and more people understand the partial nature of the truths that photography tells, and also that the context in which we see a photograph can alter its meaning (whether, for example in the *Sun*, on a gallery wall or in a school textbook).

The value of captions and text in interpreting, anchoring or changing what information we get from a photograph is also more readily accepted. Used with words, photographs can go beyond showing how things look to explaining the reasons and complexities behind them. Nevertheless, when we censure press photographers for their brash and insistent style we should remember that they are under pressure from a large public. They work with skill at high speed, to tight deadlines because most of us expect to see, almost instantly, dramatic pictures of events and people we hear about.

A large percentage of the information we glean about the world comes through our eyes and much of our view of the wider world comes from images on TV, film and in newspapers. This can give us an often incomplete, limited or one-sided vision. Some things, subjects or people, never get recorded – or very rarely. A visitor from outer space studying our media would get a very odd, unbalanced idea of our world from photographs. Few women on earth and most of those young and half naked? Black people? Mainly confined to sports, entertainment or starving. People with disabilities, gays and lesbians, the elderly, well-adjusted teenagers – do they exist? Searching the world's press one would hardly believe it.

When I first took pictures in Africa in the late 1960s, I included many pictures of women standing around looking 'decorative'. Most photographs of African women up to this period recorded them only as exotic fodder for colour supplements and coffee-table books, or else as emaciated victims of famine and violence. Under the pressure of feminism, black politics and personal experience, my own consciousness changed. I understood things differently, saw them differently and eventually photographed them differently.

This sequence of pictures illustrates how the changing consciousness of the photographer influences the choice of subject matter or the way certain subjects are shown.

above left
Ethiopia, 1967.

above right
Rwanda, 1980.

opposite
Burkina Faso, 1980.

By the end of the 1970s I was showing African and Indian women working in the fields, or carrying loads of water, wood or bricks. These women didn't suddenly start doing manual work, they had always done it. In Africa women do 60 to 80 per cent of the agricultural work plus the cooking, all the household chores and look after the children. People like me had only just begun to realise this. I had been as guilty as anyone else of devaluing women's work and ignoring their central contributions to their own economies. Men frequently, and kindly, demonstrated how things were done – hoeing, sorting, stacking, carrying. Meanwhile, until I learned to ask, women and children carried on with all their everyday tasks, unrecorded, somewhere else.

Photography is essentially a process of selection – which camera, film, viewpoint, lens and angle? But, first, which subject and how to show it? At this point many subjects or aspects of subjects fall by the wayside. They simply never, or rarely, get selected for photography. Hence the invisibility of so many groups and issues in our communications-mad society. Hence also the importance of all sorts of people getting access to training and equipment to enable them to take a part in showing their own lives.

All this has led me to try to ensure that I think carefully about

Ford machinists strike for equal pay, 1985. Several users tried or succeeded in reproducing this photograph with the two women on the left-hand side cropped off, thus making the involvement of black women invisible.

who I am including in my photographs and who I am leaving out, and why. The next step is to gain some control or influence over how the pictures are used, how they are cropped and captioned. Individuals you have carefully included may be unceremoniously chopped off 'to fit a space' or 'improve the composition'. The point you were making and the person you deliberately included end up together in the bin. In addition, the meaning you intended to convey in a photograph may be undermined or changed by a caption or related article. It takes constant thought, straight questions and occasionally a stroppy attitude to deal with this.

These concerns are given an added edge by the growth of new technology. Images can be taken, stored and transmitted at high speed round the world using computer-based techniques. It has always been possible to manipulate and change photographs using montage and retouching. Backgrounds can be altered, cigarettes removed, extra people dropped in or out, monochrome pictures finished in full colour. Now, using computer software, we can do all this and more, constructing and changing images undetectably and

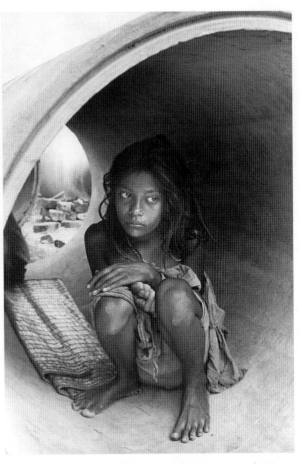

Cropping can alter the information a picture gives. Text can reinforce inaccurate information. Several pictures or a series may be necessary to give a full version of a situation. The girl in these pictures was a refugee living in a drainpipe on the outskirts of Calcutta. She had fled from east Pakistan, now Bangladesh, during the border war of 1971. The drainpipes were standing on a swamp area which was awaiting drainage so that it could be used as a building site.

This sequence is reproduced from *Macdonald Guidelines 'Photography'*

ANC branch meeting, Azania (South Africa), 1990.

on a far greater scale. When John Heartfield made his 1930s montages he wanted us to realise that they were made using paste and scissors to illustrate specific ideas. Today's advertisements and editorial columns give us seamless, impossible photos hot off the computer which give no clue as to how they were arrived at or how many sources they incorporate.

To return to basics. All photography uses light. The photo-journalist's major concern is still whether there is enough of it to make an exposure and record whatever she thinks it is important to show. She must learn many skills and struggle to make pictures which are visually exciting. Only then will others be drawn to look at them and to consider the information offered. It is a hard trick to pull off – taking interesting pictures, surviving in the world of work and trying in a small way to explain people to people without giving inaccurate, untrue or biased accounts. And I, for one, often feel more like a juggler than a photographer.

joan solomon

interrogating the holiday snap

I spent this morning washing a little Persian rug. Running my
brush back and forth across it, watching the water getting dirtier
and the colours emerging, I began to wonder who had made this
artifact. Was it a woman? Were there several women? Were
children involved? Were they singing the pattern? How many
fingers had twisted and knotted? What had they earned for doing
it? How had they displayed their wares for sale? Where had I
bought it? I thought of the holiday snaps I have of street vendors
and markets, very picturesque, often exotic, and frequently I've
bought their offerings. Their wares, I thought, were my souvenirs;
my souvenirs, their survival. Such is the nature of tourism. For
countries which rely on it, our holiday is their subsistence.

The convention of holiday photography has as its obvious
purpose the recording of a holiday, so that the pictures we take of
that holiday use as a backdrop the places we visit. We sit, stand, lie
down in front of, or lean against, monuments, towers, chateaux,
bridges, coastlines or village greens. What are we wanting from this
holiday: a rest, adventure, excitement, romance or simply a desire
for something unfamiliar? We capture the 'otherness' of cultures
through which we pass like dragonflies with our feet barely
touching the surface. What we know of other places comes to us
largely through images, films, television, travel brochures,
newspapers and perhaps some far-off history and geography
lessons. From the travel brochures and posters come a set of
idealisations. They talk of weather, scenery, cuisine, beautiful
beaches, quaint villages and usually give a glamorised history. The
way we 'learn' of local people is through the stereotypes we have
already absorbed from their endless repetition in all areas of
representation. On offer, then, from those who peddle holidays, is a
space in which to project our fantasies. Along with the luggage
we're taking we carry, in the corners of our mind, symbols of the

**He cleans the
plane that takes
us there.**

culture we're visiting. Before we've loaded our cameras we'll find, if it's France, that Frenchman in his beret with his wine and baguette – and so much the better if he's on his bike! It is for what lies lodged in our imagination that we go seeking.

We know there's more to it than this. Of the self-same countries which host our holiday Arcadias come the construction of other realities conveyed by other discourses. From 'the news' in papers, or on television, come images showing struggle, revolution, poverty and ignorance. We know that all these places have histories as complex as our own and that all these people have lives running the same gamut of emotions and needs as ours, but our holiday snaps reflect none of this; indeed we would perhaps not go where all this turmoil was glaringly evident. How countries courting tourists keep their difficulties out of sight is a story on its own.

On a personal level we are highly selective in what we photograph. As that yearly holiday pause comes round, biting a chunk out of our working lives, deadlines must be met, loose ends tied, chores long overdue done before we go away; arrangements must be made for animals to be cared for and plants to be kept alive, in addition to the paraphernalia of booking tickets, buying insurance and packing. All this is stressful. Perhaps the stress will take its toll. Will we be ill when we get there, have an accident? Let's start again with a different scenario. No stress this time, just pure pleasure. Everything has been smoothly organised. There's been time to shop for a new bathing suit, a new pair of shorts and some sandals and take in lunch with a friend. Will any of the stress or enjoyment of these preparations appear in the packet of holiday pictures? Somehow we edit all this out, photographing places without their texture and our lives as if layers of experience did not exist.

Back come the pictures from the processor, two-dimensional fragments from the outer reaches of our lives. We will share them with friends, then keep them to link us back to moments which we can gild and gild again with fantasy the further we move from them. Why, I ask myself, do I take these pictures? The answer is that I need to remember what has fascinated, moved and delighted me, for memory is a way of making meaning matter. Paradoxically, in the very moment of grasping the significance of that meaning comes the realisation of its transience. This insight evokes the anxiety of loss and the need to freeze and keep these instants. There is the feeling that I will have passed this way but once, mapping myself across other cultures. I am trying to hold the moments of myself, in the throes of wonderment at how superb and varied the world can be and at the whole strangeness of 'being' and 'witnessing'; like an Alice through my own looking-glass.

top
**Beautiful pools
are welcome on
sweltering days.**

bottom
**She has no
running water in
her home.**

'Witnessing' creates a kind of double vision running through my holiday idyll. On the one hand there's the plenitude of my holiday and then there is the condition of other people's lives. Only a fraction of either will appear in my pictures; only a fraction of the fraction I experience and see. Take the day I spent recently in Faro.

The centre of this small Portuguese town is newish and orientated round tourists. There are cafes, souvenir shops and smart boutiques. I decided to leave all that and walk into the residential area with its spacious houses and exuberant little gardens. The excitement of a day like this is simply taking my camera. It is like going with a friend who is taking me to meet the world for the first time. I am full of curiosity and expectation.

It was a very simple church that I saw, but as soon as I had pushed open the door and stepped into its quiet, I knew that this was a moment that would go unrecorded. Quite belying the simplicity of the rest of the church, what faced me was a wall gleaming with gilt, lit by one shaft of sunlight which slanted across from a side window. The rest of the small place was suffused with a soft, cool light that accentuated its simplicity. Three elderly women, dressed entirely in black from their headscarves to their shoes, were sitting absolutely still on a bench along the wall near where I had entered. All were facing what looked like a child's cot surrounded by flurries of white lace. Propped against it were three bouquets of bright vermilion gladioli. It took me a moment to grasp what was happening. I caught my breath and stood transfixed at the sight of the small dead child. And so I stood, neither going into the church, nor going out, simply stood behind the velvet dark of my closed eyes until I slid away and out of the church and up along the road and the next and the next, wrapped in thought. Later that afternoon I fruitlessly combed the area trying to find the church again. I knew that I would never intrude on those women to take the picture I so badly wanted, but somehow I needed to be there. At that time and in that place I had no way of representing the moment of my holiday that had most profoundly moved me. The reality we construct is only ever partial.

Will tourists, I wonder, ever record homeless British youth sleeping in the streets? Our photographs never convey the personal, ideological, political and economic conditions stalking the underbelly of our holiday 'wonderland'.

There is a vast pervasive consumer ideology with its expensive technology implicit in the production of pictures. This process supports multi-million-pound industries from the manufacture of cameras, processors, enlargers, chemicals and so on, to the printing and publishing involved in advertising the holiday and the holiday snap. All this is much less visible than the hungry eyes of 'locals' holding out their trinkets to tourists.

An awareness of the disparity between ourselves, who have the holiday and record it; the tourist and photographic industries, which build empires from our need to play and our attempt to defeat transience, and the 'locals', whose livelihoods depend on our ability to spend, puts the holiday snap into a different perspective.

A wonderland for sightseers.

nilofar akmut

mapping ourselves

As with most oral cultures, stories surrounding the lives and times of our ancestors were recounted to us as children huddled around a matriarch. Ours wasn't a tale tenderly woven or embroidered into the fabric of women involved in the beautification of their homes and themselves – far from it. Some families, like my ancestors, due to their economic circumstances and a violent social history, had little inclination or time to follow traditional patterns.

I can never claim to have a complete knowledge of my family's history. Apart from the complexity, deep painful silences surrounded the fearful traumas inflicted on their lived reality. What I can hope to achieve is an understanding for myself and I look to images in order to articulate pictorially those deliberately misplaced moments of our history. For this I have to look beyond our family album and enter the realms of public photography. This perceives itself as objectively documenting anonymous characters and situations on a world stage bereft of individual emotional contact. What I find there are generalised images of our art and culture; images of war, well-known photojournalistic triumphs like that of Gandhi appearing to share a joke with the Mountbattens. Shreds of our history are represented as depicting our meaning and much is left unsaid. Too much of what I know to be my history is concealed and none of those generalised images are my images.

For me our story begins with my great-grandmother, who was a widow by the time she was 20 years of age. She was married at 14 and had three children. On her husband's death her idyllic lifestyle came to an abrupt end. Embroidery became a means to support her family, preferable to being dependent on her late husband's family. An illiterate woman herself, she attended meticulously to her daughter's education, ensuring her a respectable profession in education.

On the partition of India in August 1947, members of my family were thrown into turmoil and conflict regarding migration. Each of them had to make the difficult decision of opting for Pakistan because of the demarcation of new borders. Families were torn apart as extreme demands of changing affiliation were made by the state and warring factions. Some refused to leave until forcibly ejected and arrived in groups or as individuals in trying circumstances, stateless, jobless and homeless – refugees.

Departing with their lives and a stitch on their backs, the daughters and granddaughters of the household crossed over into Pakistan, fleeing in a cattle train pursued by daggers in the hands of Hindus and Sikhs who, till the day before, had been their neighbours and friends. They were never to return to their homes. Some never recovered. Others, disillusioned by the state to which they had been loyal and which had rejected their political and economic contributions, remained in a constant state of exile, developing conflicting identities in both fantasy and reality.

Both my paternal and maternal families endured an enforced state of exile. Though circumstances in each instance were different, the common factor informing their lives was colonialism. They passed on their perpetual migrant status to my generation, and the families are now torn apart and lives are lived across the various continents in the world. Our loyalties and identities are further fragmented and we find ourselves in the unbearable position of not feeling assimilated in any culture. Insufficiently eastern or western, our conflicting and multi-faceted identities are striving to create new ones as we defy simplistic stereotyping or ethnic descriptions and designations for ourselves.

We need new images to reveal and help us to find out who we are. I myself need to make them. Here, my image is a representation of a particular moment which ensured the continuation of my family's creative energy. These legs represent not only the rape and pillage of the Indian subcontinent, but also the protection offered to the womenfolk escaping from possible execution. In spite of being permanently cut off from their roots, the women continued a history of unending struggle politically and intellectually, which was to affect another generation of women, one to which I myself belong. I continue with installations and my camera to uncover the painful silences in our history.

we have nothing to lose but our invisibility

As a rebellion against family politics and media bias, I recommend the camera. That's why I take it with me to events that get little press coverage – particularly when trouble-free. My parents never went to demos. Come to think of it, the general impression within the family about demonstrators was that they were all a bit potty. Neither Mum nor Dad thought much of the protests that were made against the siting of the US Polaris submarine base at the Holy Loch, just down the Clyde coast from the hotel that Dad had bought in 1944, with money borrowed from a fellow freemason in Glasgow. Their prejudice was echoed on a camp site in north Norfolk in the early 1960s, when my new husband and I stuck a CND pennant near our small ridge tent. A passing camper pointed it out to his children with a drawled 'Look at those people: they've got a mini car, a mini tent and mini minds!' A real opinion-former he, his educated timbre penetrated the canvas walls. And we, still enthusing about the latest Aldermaston march, wondered which newspaper he had been reading.

My dad read the *Daily Express* all his life. His anti-union opinions were constantly reinforced by its shirkers-and-traitors line. That daily dose of tabloid reading, illustrated by carefully chosen photographic 'evidence', is prepared for our consumption by masters of assorted genres, sponsored by advertisers. In my middle age I have rebelled against both the politics of my family (they were perfect Thatcherites) and media bias. In consequence I now use my camera as a weapon.

It began in the 1980s in Woodford Green, where we live, on the fringes of London's east end. I got involved, inspired by the idea that 'Greenham women are everywhere', in organising events to publicise the existence of a local women's peace group. We decided to focus on Sylvia Pankhurst's largely ignored anti-aerial bombing monument: a stone bomb on top of a stone plinth, almost hidden from view by forest trees. This marked the failure of the World Disarmament Conference in 1932 to prohibit the use of bombing planes against civilian targets, and the subsequent attacks using mustard gas against the people, livestock and land of Ethiopia.

My childhood had been haunted by my father's recollection of the Turkish policy of genocide directed against Armenians. No doubt, bright lad that he was, he had read about this crime in... the newspapers. My younger brother and I were regularly instructed, throughout the second world war, to eat up our dinners while thinking of 'the starved Armenians'. I expect Dad felt sorry for the Abyssinians as well. It wasn't until I discovered something of the monument's history that I realised that Miss Pankhurst had not only lived in the area for 32 years, emigrating to Africa with her son in 1956, but that she herself had gone to no end of trouble to draw the attention of the British public to the plight of Ethiopia (renamed Abyssinia) and its exiled emperor in the wake of Italian fascist ambitions. To this day, no Italian national has been charged with war crimes in connection with atrocities committed during Mussolini's campaign against black Africans. Sylvia even published a weekly newspaper for many years, edited in her Woodford home and printed on local presses, which she called New Times and Ethiopia News. Occasionally she would use horrific photographs sent to her of mutilated and dead Ethiopians to break through the smokescreen of indifference with a barrage of demands for 'social justice'. The Foreign Office opened a special file entitled: 'How to answer letters from Miss Sylvia Pankhurst'.

Friends and supporters of the peace cause breathed life into this old near-forgotten history, once a hot news item. We gathered in the vicinity of the stone bomb for annual picnics and junkets which included morris dancing (which Sylvia enjoyed and painted pictures of) and a choir singing Dame Ethel Smyth's suffragette anthem, 'March of the Women'. One Hiroshima Day, a local Greenham woman, Maggie Freake, re-unveiled the monument. My friend Beryl was a dab hand at whipping out her Boots 110 camera on these occasions. It dangled from her wrist wherever we took the peace banner. To begin with, I had relied on black and white photos from the press to illustrate the record I kept in an ever-expanding album showing the who, where, what and when of our resistance to the 'defence' policies of the British state, as the presence of Cruise missiles escalated anxieties about health – not least from the hazards attached to radiation from nuclear technologies. Then one year, to our surprise, we were spied upon by an overly friendly protester lookalike, who photographed everyone, claiming that as an unemployed man it was one way of eking out his benefit – only for him to vanish without ever trying to sell any pictures to us. We saw him once again at an anti-apartheid rally in the days of the free

Nelson Mandela campaign, recording the moment when policemen's helmets were knocked off in Trafalgar Square by well-aimed bottles and cans.

That did it! Infuriated by the direction of the sponsored gaze, and its marketable motive, I bought my own 110 camera and set about making and keeping a private record of resistance, taking advantage of the civil liberties afforded to us by our Hyde Park Corner democracy. This instrument remains my safety valve for disaffection. I am temperamentally disposed to follow in the footsteps of the suffragists, or constitutionalists, who demanded votes for women without having recourse to violence. Suffragettes, while they did not all embrace the view that violence against property (Emmeline Pankhurst called it 'the argument of the broken window pane') was the only way to keep 'the cause' in the news, nonetheless participated in some spectacularly destructive acts. Not least of these was a form of protest used by Sylvia Pankhurst against her own body's needs. She martyred herself through hunger, thirst and sleep strikes, co-ordinating her releases from prison when her health broke down with daring and illegal appearances at public meetings in the east end, challenging the status quo. The suffragists, on the other hand, challenged with decorum, emphasising the diversity of women's talents and skills,

confident of the rightness and relevance of our inclusion on the voting register. But though there is nothing spectacular in the clicking of a camera's shutter for personal and political reasons, it remains nonetheless a way to chronicle resistance to and protest against the continuous representations of 'what is going on' in an ideological framework not of our making.

The resultant images I select are evidence of a consensual reality shared with countless others. This bias cannot be broken or captured for posterity through a past recollected by using the selection techniques of the traditional family album and snapshots, with their illusions of 'how things were'. Nor is it sufficiently newsworthy to count frequently in column or headline, though we can reflect on what has been rendered well-nigh invisible at the British Museum's newspaper library in Colindale – a time-consuming process to say the least. As an alternative, I would urge the reader/photographer to record and provide a related text for a shared present that so instantly becomes a shared past. Such thoughts have set me to reflecting on the fate of my own photographic inheritance, and what I have already lost.

After the deaths of my parents, their photograph albums vanished. The few family photos that have survived to come into my hands tell me nothing of resistance and everything about compliance with a set of social rules. It worries me that so much is lost, not only because of the lack of awareness of the value of domestically based photographic records, but also because of the narrow range of possibilities explored in them. This experience has made me very conscious of how important it is to make and keep a record of life as I see it. This is completed with explanatory text so that no one can be in any doubt as to the meanings, as far as I am concerned, of subjects and objectives, of who and what and where they are. Not for me the mere reliance upon the enterprise and initiatives of high-street photographers, the annual school portraits religiously collected, the high days and holidays enjoyed with family and friends.

My own rebellion lies in deciding to expand the range of issues consciously addressed with camera and journal beyond the personal and private to include chronicling of events, recording opinions shared, accounting for feelings and emotions aroused. This is my way of insisting on a continuing currency of ideas and ideals ignored as irrelevant to the agendas of politics, or different from those I was encouraged to embrace by influential and powerful sources, beginning with my family. It is a process I recommend others to explore. It neither damages the health nor depends on substantial amounts of cash or talent. 'Join us,' as

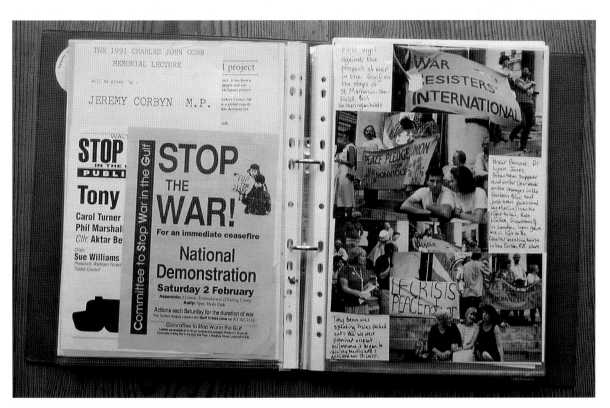

Emmeline Pankhurst used to say, addressing enormous audiences of enthusiastic women in the Royal Albert Hall and at other gatherings throughout the land before the great war escalated the demise of civil liberties. We have nothing to lose but our collective and individual invisibility.

One last word: eventually all my albums will be passed on to my daughter Emma, who is already compiling her own. I must say, were there to be a proliferation of social albums, what interesting contexts they would provide for the discussion of the impact of personality on politics: and vice versa! I get the feeling that Emma is trying to throw off the chains of her political upbringing in order to find her own voice in debate. This she will no doubt illustrate through selective photography.

working in groups

beryl graham

mothers of invention

This is a story about the telling of stories; of some particular stories which are only a small part of a larger tale of change. The telling of contemporary stories in a region where histories are often in the dangerous territory of nostalgia.

In outlining a 'behind-the-scenes' story of how an exhibition came together, I hope that it may be useful to anyone wanting to try something similar. The results will always be different, though, because the stories are always different.

To introduce the 'characters': your narrator is a full-time arts worker – young, childless, white, middle class and northern. I'm a photography organiser for a media arts organisation, at the time of the project called Newcastle Media Workshop.

The second character is Rosy Thornton from Walker Health Project, who had worked with the group for some time, then worked with us all throughout our weekly sessions, very usefully suggesting ways of working which would suit the group best. Walker is one of several locally based health projects in priority areas, which take an admirably wide view of health, from confidence-building to drop-in 'health shops'.

Welbeck Road School Mothers and Toddlers Group are, of course, the key characters in the story. They were a group of about 12 local women who all had older children at the school, were 20 to 40ish, and had been meeting twice a week (once a week with Rosy) for some time. As a group they were very strong, meeting up often outside the school, organising for themselves trips, socials, bingo and so on. With some help from Rosy they had successfully applied for a grant for toys for their creche. Within their own realm, they were very witty and quite confident; at points outside that, those familiar conspiracies of class and gender made them very uncertain.

As a landscape for a story, Walker itself lacks those picturesque

terraced houses which attract gentrification and film-makers, but it is certainly northern, working class and suffers from the familiar post-ship-building ills. It is also situated in the specific histories of the north-east. The traditionally very separate roles of men's and women's work makes the questioning of those roles fraught with problems, where unemployment literally 'unmans' with the shift from heavy engineering to light industrial and low-paid 'women's work'. There may be a certain amount of matriarchy within the home, but the dominant visual representations of work have been of men's work. How can you make pictures of 'women's work' as valuable? Can some stories both celebrate women and persuade men that doing such work will not destroy their own identity?

The project developed a long time ago when a plan to tour Jo Spence's exhibition, 'The Picture of Health', to local health projects revealed the possibility of doing some practical work as a preparation for the exhibition itself. Lengthy talks with the health projects firmed up what might be possible and what we would want from the work (any arts organisation claiming to be a 'mere facilitator' is, I think, stretching credibility a bit). We wanted a 'product' which we could distribute and which would, we hoped, encourage other women's groups to try something along the same lines. It should look reasonable and be easily distributable; it should encourage 'constructed' ways of working, informed by some of Jo Spence's methods. It should try to bridge the credibility gap which is widening to match the economic one between north and south – it's definitely a tough job to persuade local community groups that work produced south of Birmingham is relevant to them at all.

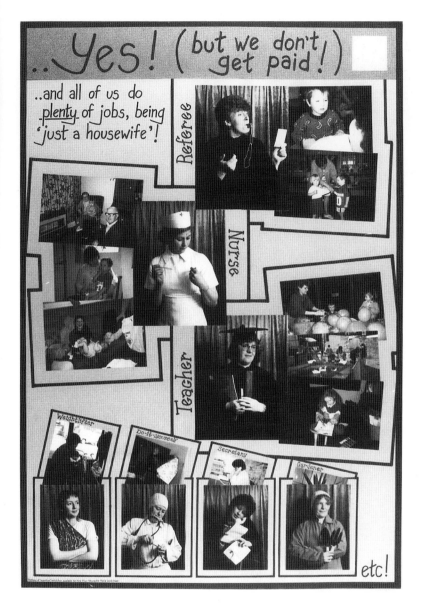

Initially we used simple colour snapshots from which it was easier to make montages to tell our stories. This, I thought, would also be an accessible way in for future photographic practice in the women's group. With hindsight, this choice proved essential to forming a familiar base on which to build without losing the women's fragile confidence.

The time scale, from starting research to the finished exhibition, was around nine months. What follows is a broad outline of the stages in this particular story, which contains useful pointers for others who might wish to undertake this kind of project.

Research, money-raising and forming a group

This was probably the longest and most difficult part. It took a couple of days a week over about eight weeks.

Money is the root of all exhibitions, so you need to get advice from your local arts, education and community organisations. As it was a 'key' project, we supplied some money from our budgets, but I also tried to raise contributions from photographic suppliers and colour snap processors. I failed to get even a decent discount, mostly because I hadn't realised what a long and persistent task it was; also because I couldn't show them exactly what the end product was, and because they didn't seem too keen on the 'women's group' bit (children yes, women no).

The health project contributed £100 to the overall budget. As a rough guide, altogether we used 18 colour films (36 exposures), with two sets of prints from each, and about 20 black and white films. We used about 25 sheets of rough, and 40 sheets of smart layout paper. The laminating cost was £50 – very cheap – and the travelling case about £20. There was lots of photocopying for publicity. I hired a teacher's costume from a fancy dress shop.

Research and forming a group tend to happen at the same time as trying to find out what is feasible and suitable and will depend on the interests and the group. This project would certainly have been very different without such a lively, talented and committed bunch. Once they had decided that they would be interested in doing it, nearly all of them turned up to every session. They would definitely have said if they weren't interested: sometimes I think that community groups end up doing projects just because they feel sorry for the hapless-looking arts workers! Please don't get too disappointed if your group should peter out, or flag, or take much longer. I consider myself very lucky to have been working with such a dynamic combination of people.

Working with the group

I was introduced to the group by Rosy on one of their occasional girls' nights out and took along a compact camera which we could all use. Taking the prints along to the first session proved to be a good ice-breaker and a recurring theme in the project. Photographs are a way of sociable sharing which fitted in very well with the group's way of working, helping us to swap very different stories. Above all it was fun.

We met for 16 sessions over eight months, with breaks for school holidays and the odd other session like swimming, to prevent boredom. Most weeks there was a creche, and we were able to work in another room, although some toddlers wouldn't stay in the creche for more than a few minutes. Sometimes the creche went missing, and we worked knee-deep in toddlers – not recommended for a whole project. Once the kids were settled(ish), and we'd wound down with a game of bingo, the sessions were about an hour long, which seemed about right.

We started off the first session by looking at family albums, 'baby mags', and self-portraits, asking, 'How can you tell things about people from pictures? What things are missing?' We went through how to use the compact 35mm cameras with autofocus and built-in flash, and as everyone was itching to use them, the group took the cameras home with a brief to 'take pictures of things which are very important to you – good or bad; things which don't usually get photographed'. The women shared one camera between two, and used either the self-timer or family and friends when they wanted pictures of themselves.

In the gap during which the photographs were being processed we found a useful time to look at more pictures, in this case photos of 'work' and picture stories.

Getting the photographs back was, of course, the best bit. Everyone opened their own packets, had the chance to remove any

they didn't want to show, and after the initial uproar, each person, including Rosy and me, 'talked through' their pictures one by one. We had two sets printed, so that people could keep their own, leaving one set for the exhibition. It is cheaper to get two sets printed at the start if working with a through-the-post colour processing company.

The second brief was to 'take a day in the life of anything: you, somebody else, anything'. These two briefs formed the basis of the whole exhibition, with the odd reshoot and extra picture needed.

From here on the project was a process of selection and organisation, starting off with each woman doing her own A3 panel in rough first, sticking photos to sugar paper. They selected pictures for their 'importance', their story-telling and their suitability for public display. Some told stories, some picked out key images, and one woman decided on relevant song titles, including 'I Never Promised You a Rose Garden'. Once persuaded of the necessity to choose only a few photographs out of many, their choices were fairly self-sufficient.

Writing the captions was where some of the women suddenly lost confidence and their flair with words, no doubt remembering bad school experiences. It was here that recalling what people had said as they 'talked through' their pictures was very useful, and with help from me and each other we worked it out. Using a tape-recorder at that earlier stage might prove invaluable, though initially inhibiting.

Having said something about themselves individually, what else did they want to say? The larger panels in the exhibition were worked on by assorted groups of three to four. These panels included one of 'the group' – what it had achieved, what they did and so on; one on 'Walker' – what it had, what it needed, and one named 'The Giro-Cycle' in a flash of inspiration from Carol, which grew from Linda's 'Day in the life of where the money goes'.

The 'Do you work?' pair of panels we all worked on together, with me being fairly directive. We listed the paid equivalents of 'housework', the props needed to signify these jobs, and decided who would bring in what and who would play what. In the next session, I brought in a simple flash head and brolly, and we set up the shots, with much laughter and much confusion of toddlers seeing their mothers transformed.

It would have been nice to have then taken the group through the processes of black and white printing, but school summer holidays were looming, so I borrowed a darkroom and printed them myself.

The final part was setting out a series of small panels which visually outlined the 'behind-the-scenes' story of how we made the exhibition. We had all the panels laid out and captioned in rough before I took them to do the final layout, having decided on colours and style. This took me forever, so I can recommend getting someone who has got a bit of design talent to do this if at all possible. You need to get advice about layout if you are going to laminate your exhibition, as this affects spacing and other factors.

After a final approval from the group, the exhibition was laminated. I'd advise you to scout around local community resources first, as commercially it can be expensive. I also bought a lightweight travelling case and made a photocopyable poster blank, and, most importantly, some good exhibition details and publicity. Don't forget press prints and press releases as part of the process: what impression do you want to give of the work? Distribution is very important, but is also the point where people begin to lose interest. As a result, many fantastic community-based projects don't get the exposure they deserve, so it's best to bear this in mind at the design stage so that publicity material can be distributed with as little effort as possible.

The exhibition has so far been to libraries, art galleries and conferences, and I keep the group mailed on press coverage. We also troop along if there's something special like the Lord Mayor opening it, or a chance of encouraging local women's groups. The exhibition has been successful in this aim: as a direct result two similar projects have been started up, one with young women probationers and one with a girls' youth club, so we hope this snowballing effect will continue. In relation to the sheer number of people reached, however, exhibitions are never as good as getting into print, so if you sniff a chance, grab it!

As a fairly inexperienced arts worker, I learned an awful lot from

Shirley: Monday Blues (pay bills all day!)

off to the post office...

...to cash my books and pay the gas...

Mother + daughter enjoy a quiet cuppa

...to pay the electric (another bill)

...and try to do some shopping

...a bus, then a metro to town...

STEP FOR MORE WINTER S...

Step this way? — easier said than done!

just window shopping— dream kitchen...

...back to reality!

the project, such as when it is possible to be 'directive' without cramping others' ideas. In this project it was in the areas of overall plan, overall design, and in providing something firm to start off on, with a quick 'result'. Being too 'undirective' at first, I discovered, doesn't seem to help people with little confidence in their own talents. Looking at the exhibition, all the best, most unpredictable and creative parts came directly from the women themselves, built around my rather worthy outline.

Above all, the project convinced me that the difficult theory base of contemporary gallery photography, which I deal with as part of my job, is in fact relevant to community-based work. Questions of language and experience are of course different, but this project does work with narrative, juxtaposition and simple role-playing, as well as with the talent of visually representing the abstract.

The stories this exhibition tells are, of course, partial accounts of a bigger set of stories. They're specifically white working class, specifically Walker 1988, and not particularly questioning of gender roles. Perhaps stories should always be read alongside other stories.

This is my story of how the exhibition got together. If you asked someone else who was involved, well, theirs would be a different story.

The exhibition, by Welbeck Road School Mothers and Toddlers Group, Projects UK (formerly Newcastle Media Workshops) and Walker Health Project, was shown at Welbeck School and Newcastle Central Library, among other local community venues; the Cockpit Gallery in London; and other small galleries or conferences in Leeds, Birmingham, Stockport, Glasgow and Bootle.

When the public darkroom facilities of Projects UK opened, women from the Welbeck Road Mothers Group participated in another photography project with Kaye Oliver, this time using SLR cameras and printing their own black and white photographs about self-image. They were still involved in photography projects when Projects UK was closed down in 1992.

Welbeck Road School Mothers and Toddlers Group:
Carole Ure, Helen Monaghan, Susan Searle, Shirley Rutherford, Linda Murphy, Yvonne McAlinden, Janice Munroe, Susan Smith, Yvonne Storey, Shirley Barber.
Walker Health Project: Rosy Thornton

'give me a camera and i'll show you how i feel'

The Cockpit Cultural Studies team used photography with young people for around ten years. They had a large teaching darkroom and a studio with electronic flash which were available for use by groups of young people and their teachers or supervisors. They also established working methods with groups which enabled them to go beyond the youth club session model and use photography for productions (whether books or exhibitions) of a high standard.

In 1984, a local hostel for homeless young people started sessions with the Cockpit as part of its activity programme. The emphasis was on getting the young residents busy and active and

thus breaking the cycle of unemployment and lethargy which the organisation identified as being a disabling feature of homelessness. Sessions got residents 'out of the building' and off the hands of the hostel staff team, who often bore the brunt of the boredom and frustration.

Young people joining the photography group for the first time were cautious. They did not mind taking the pictures but were afraid to be photographed themselves, saying that they had never seen a good picture of themselves. Within two sessions they had at least one image they were pleased with and identified with.

Once this happened they would produce them at an alarming rate. It soon became clear that photographs played a useful role in helping the young women and men to assert their sense of identity and place at an otherwise chaotic and sometimes disturbed time in their lives. Photographs presented positive images of an up-to-date self, a new person established in his or her own right at a distance from the recent past with its traumas of family upheaval and homelessness. The pictures located them in a new social context, amongst their friends and engaging in new interests.

I was one of the workers involved in a project which led to the 'Down But Not Out' exhibition. Spike is one of the hostel residents. Here she comments on her involvement and what the work meant to her in that exhibition as a young photographer:

For some time residents from the hostel had been using the facilities of the Cockpit as part of a photography session that was run by the cultural studies team in co-ordination with the hostel's education programme. We felt that we could do something more with the sessions, so with all the negatives we already had and plans to take more pictures we set about discussing a structure for an exhibition.

When I was at home I didn't have a good camera so I didn't take photography that seriously. The pictures I did then were just scenes: shots of outside, and that was it, basically. And then one day when I was at the hostel someone asked me to come along to the Cockpit and take some pictures. I didn't like being photographed but they simply refused to let me take pictures for the whole of the session, so I had to give a bit, just saying, 'Right, I'll mess around a bit and you can take some pictures of me. You say what you want me to do and I'll do it. Then you pose for me.'

It was just a bit of a muck-around and sort of learning to use the studio, but it's funny to look back at those pictures and see how much I've changed. I suppose it's a bit of a novelty to see yourself, and there were just so many pictures. It was the start of me using the studio and beginning to work out sessions.

In the years that the Cockpit worked with the hostel, young women's involvement was consistently high.

There was a picture of me taken in my old room when I was first at the hostel right next to another picture I had on the wall. When you photocopy your own photograph and blow it up, it looks like a movie poster and I was really into that. If I was going to be in a picture I'd prefer to tamper with it a bit.

I always insist that I don't appear in front of the camera. I'm not a model. I insist that I'm the photographer. There is obviously a real difference between being in front of the camera and being behind it.

The studio is really good. If you're in a room taking photos you make the best out of what you can in the room, but you can make the studio into what you want it to be. I'll plan out a photo session and know exactly who I want to be in the picture because I know the idea will suit that particular person's face. I can actually visualise what the picture's going to look like with him or her in it.

Sometimes pictures would play a role in patching up differences with the family left behind. Photos were sent home to prove that people could cope, that they were well and that their parents need not worry or to say: 'Look, this is the version of me that you wouldn't acknowledge or approve of, and I'm proud of it.'

Those residents who really cued into the sessions would soon have their own impressive collection of photos in an album or box and the photographs taped to their bedroom walls helped to define their private space, a crucial need when you share a room with a fellow resident. Clearly, in the context of ruptured family and institutional backgrounds and an insecure future, a bank of positive personal images provided a strong point of anchorage and an alternative to the family album that they had stepped from, or had been catapulted out of.

> There are a few pictures of me when I was ten or 11, but most of them are up to the age of five. They're all really nice ones, but after that I just simply refused to have a picture taken. I don't think people mind so much having photographs of themselves when they're little. I'm more worried about seeing pictures of me now, because I'm more critical of myself.
>
> I suppose every parent wants some sort of picture of the little one, really just something sweet to remember how she was – you know, the age of innocence. It hits you when you become a teenager and you go through puberty and things like that. It's like your life changes around and you start to have real positive feelings and thoughts for yourself and become sensitive; you start to worry about your appearance, about opinions, and things matter more as you grow older, and you begin to realise a lot of things.
>
> I'm fed up with being asked, 'How do you feel about what you do? What are your views on homelessness?' You have all these media people saying let's make a video about you or let's do some pictures or something about homeless people. We will do it for you. Because of this you just get the urge to get up and do it yourself. I'd much rather not be interviewed on TV; not be asked, 'How do you feel about being homeless?' I'd rather someone gave me a camera and said, 'Show us how you feel.'

Throughout 1987 sessions ran for half a day a week with a core group of four or five committed residents and a large shifting and changing group who would attend irregularly. We planned activities which would raise awareness of the possible uses of the residents' photographs and talked of the way in which the media represented homeless young people. This included more studio portraiture work, montage using the photocopier and individual residents' personal panels from selections of their work. This helped establish a shared understanding of what the exhibition project should address, and of how best to use the group's photographs in a public context. Out of all this the idea for the 'Down But Not Out' exhibition was born.

I wasn't interested at first. I thought it would look rather boring – just pictures of hostel life. You can't appreciate it when you're actually living in the hostel and someone suggests the idea of making an exhibition about it. A hostel is not your idea of a home, a proper home. I didn't take it that seriously till I realised we could get more out of the exhibition.

I mean, why should a bunch of people living in the place

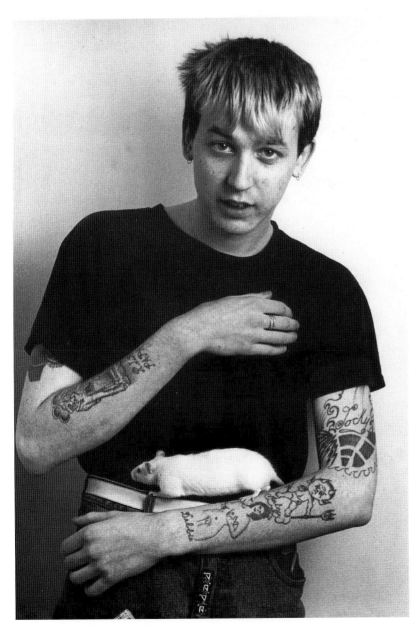

and some youth workers want to make an exhibition about young homeless people in a hostel? It was kind of a mad idea to go with and I think people were really surprised about how good it actually looked when it was finished. So people's response to it was really encouraging.

The staff felt there was a need to convince interested residents that a large-scale production was possible and that despite the work involved such a project would be fun and ultimately rewarding. The concept of a production team was introduced. This enabled the group to distinguish between those who wished to negotiate decisions and organise practical tasks and those who were simply prepared to feature in the exhibition or were just attending sessions. The production team consisted of four workers, two from the cultural studies team; the photography tutor and the education co-ordinator from the hostel; three residents and one ex-resident.

The Cockpit are people who have done this sort of work for years and years so they're well capable of pulling off an exhibition. They know what they are doing but with each new group of people it's different. We are seen as being really inexperienced and not very confident; wanting to say something and not knowing how to go about it. So we kind of needed each other: they needed us for something to make an exhibition about, we needed them to help us.

At first it felt almost as if there was no room for our thoughts, but after a while everyone did start throwing things in and people started voicing the ways in which they wanted things done. Thinking about how the exhibition was being put together, we did start to sit down as a group and have discussions, which were useful. Sometimes the workers would be authoritative, almost as if they were in charge; the ones spelling out all the ideas.

I think people were interested, but while the staff seemed full of confidence, I think everyone else was a bit 'I don't think we're gonna get that far, it's just not going to be taken seriously.' Then we went further and further into it, it became more interesting to do and we realised we were surprising ourselves and that we could make something really positive out of it.

The production team was quite a small group by the time we got nearer the end and we were really getting a chance to say how we wanted the exhibition to be done. I definitely started to take it more seriously and people like David and Malcy and Amy and I started getting really involved with it. Not in the way of saying 'This is my work' – I couldn't have pulled off something like that on my own. We all needed each other and I felt quite proud.

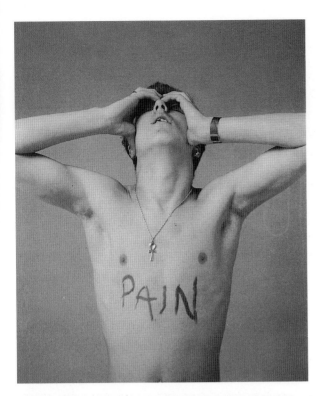

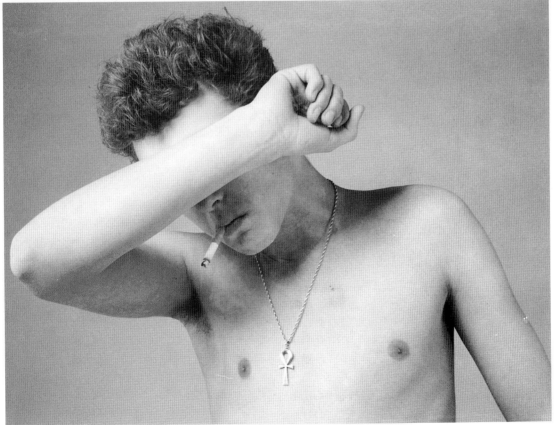

*Young people had been able to say what they wanted to,
express the situation they were in. Actually communicate
with people. It was a way of putting across to them how we
felt about the situation we were in and that we weren't going
to just sit there and take the kind of things that people were
saying to us.*

The exhibition had a series of portraits and pictures of residents in
their rooms. There were other panels which addressed residents'
feelings about how the media stereotyped homeless young people.
Another set of panels described the 'homeless circuit' with the aid
of a transformed Snakes and Ladders and Monopoly board and a
glossary of the range of professional workers that you might expect
to encounter if you became homeless.

A poster was designed and produced along with a leaflet to hand
out at the show with a selection of photos and quotations from the
main body of work, and a press release was mailed to the national
press and other relevant media.

The private launch at the Cockpit Gallery was a valuable trial
run for the show with a sympathetic group of guests in attendance.
Residents were wholeheartedly congratulated for their impressive
display, which raised their confidence in the product and prepared

them for the demanding public launch that was to come.

I think people were really surprised how good it looked when it was finished. The response to it was really brilliant. It was quite embarrassing being one of the people at the centre of attention and it felt strange being one of those responsible for the exhibition and being praised, your work being appreciated by lots of people. It feels so good to have someone tell you your work is good. It's the most rewarding thing that you can have as a photographer.

The exhibition was mounted for four days in June 1988 at King's Cross station. We chose King's Cross because it's where people often arrive when they leave home and come to London. Furthermore, we were ensured of a bigger audience in one day than the average gallery had in a year, and they would be the sort of people who wouldn't necessarily go to an exhibition like this one.

It was opened by Ken Livingstone, the residents' choice of celebrity. The press photographers were, we recognised, disappointed with the exhibition's photos. Unable to see beyond their own stereotypes, they remarked that there was nothing really about homelessness here. One of the production team had a white rat which received a disproportionate amount of attention, being put on Ken's shoulder for a photograph. (It wasn't homeless and it hadn't contributed to the exhibition!) The residents sat with their exhibition in the station for four days, encouraging people to respond to what they saw by writing in the comments book. They had some hostility but most of the responses were good. The public, used to ignoring the older homeless people who slept, begged and congregated on crates around the station, were being presented with an alternative picture of the repercussions of homelessness.

The exhibition worked in a good way and a bad way: it labelled me as being a homeless person but at the same time it also gave me the chance to defend that and actually speak out about it, because up to then I never said I lived in a hostel – I'd always told people I lived in a shared house. There is a difference between the two and it was like I'd finally started having to acknowledge that I lived in a hostel. We all had different reasons for wanting to do the exhibition. We all wanted to make the hostel sound a positive place and put ourselves over as a bunch of articulate young people. The hostel may not be an ideal place to live but it's a starting point for us and it's not that bad – at least it's a roof over our heads.

The aim of the exhibition was to challenge stereotypes of homeless people created through the media. I hate the media, as it is now anyway. The experience of making the exhibition gave me a lot of confidence, especially now, seeing all the work I did for it. I appreciate doing that more than ever, and realise how it has helped me to get work now, as well as giving me experience then. For example, I'm doing a BBC video with a friend from the hostel. It's semi-documentary but a video diary as well.

I've gone from being a shy anti-social person who hated being in a hostel and classed as homeless to being this real radical youth who was just out on her personal mission to put the world straight about homelessness.

Rufford Street Hostel houses young people from 16 to 21 years old and is run by the Alone in London service.

The Cockpit Arts Workshop was run by the Inner London Education Authority and was closed on the abolition of ILEA.

The 'Down But Not Out' exhibition can be hired out from the Leaving Home Project at Centrepoint. It has been used by various community organisations including the National Association for the Care and Rehabilitation of Offenders (NACRO), London Connection, Shelter and Alone in London.

There is also a book about this project, *Down But Not Out: Young People, Photography and Images of Homelessness*, by Andrew Dewdney, Claire Grey, Andy Minnion and the residents of Rufford Street Hostel, published by Trentham Books, 1994.

Claire Grey acknowledges the help of Andy Minnion in the interviewing for and writing of this article.

kamina walton

creating positive images:
working with primary school girls

In January 1987 I was employed by Blackfriars Photography Project to work three days a week for a term at Snowsfields Primary School near London Bridge. Blackfriars was an independent project which had been working with the local community in north Southwark for 11 years but until this time it had done very little work with the primary school age group. My brief was to explore the possible uses of photography across the school curriculum, working with first- and second-year juniors. Because of the positive responses to the work produced, Blackfriars then managed to fund-raise for a two-year programme that would enable me to continue to develop the work at Snowsfields, whilst at the same time expanding to other primary schools in the area.

During this time I was very lucky to meet and work alongside Jasmine Jayham, an enthusiastic class teacher at Snowsfields. When I first began working with her she had talked about the continuing difficulty of finding good multi-cultural resource material. She saw the opportunity, through photography, for the children to produce their own teaching resources based on their local environment and daily lives. During the two years children became familiar with the use of cameras in the classroom and were soon applying photography to a variety of curricular disciplines.

In October 1988, as part of the Spectrum Women's Photography Festival, a group of ten girls between the ages of eight and 11 were given the opportunity to participate in a girls' workshop at South London Art Gallery (run by myself and Vivienne Reiss from Blackfriars). As the workshop was limited to two hours it was decided to explore simple ideas around narrative and sequencing, together with ways of representing individual words such as 'strong' or 'angry' in a single image. This involved both studio-based and location work, and 35mm and medium-format cameras.

When the girls were asked about the words they wanted to

represent it was interesting that they all immediately wanted to portray the word 'pretty'. For all of them this meant standing with hands on hips looking directly at the camera, whereas in all the other images produced most of them averted their gaze. When looking at magazines such as *Smash Hits* we can see that these poses are a direct reflection of the way in which young girls' pop idols, such as Kylie and Dannii Minogue, are packaged by the music industry. The girls chose to identify with and recreate the pose regardless of cultural background, highlighting the lack of role models they have to choose from in the media. It is interesting to see how they went on to use photography some months later, taking control of the picture space in order to create their own positive images.

The workshop gave the girls the rare opportunity to work as a single-sex group, and time was spent at the end of the session discussing how they felt about the experience. The response was extremely positive. All the girls involved agreed that they had felt

more confident about exploring ideas, and enjoyed not having the worry of boys trying to get hold of equipment, or laughing at what they were doing.

The following term a number of the girls who had been involved in the workshop came to me and asked if they could use photography to produce some work exploring their feelings about their treatment by boys in both the classroom and the playground. They had talked about a number of things they continually experienced from boys such as physical and verbal harassment (amounting to both sexism and racism), and their domination of classroom work areas such as the computer and construction games. They not only felt their treatment was unfair, but many found it an intimidating experience.

The next stage was to discuss with Jasmine how they were going to present the issues in a series of photographs, and how captions might accompany them. One issue the group felt strongly about was that although the work was all about their conflict with boys

they did not want boys involved in the project. Therefore a way had to be found to represent rather than show boys. At this point it was suggested that the girls could use parts of their own bodies, such as hands and feet, that would imply the boys' presence in the photographs.

There were problems about taking the photos in situ: whether in the classroom or the playground it would be difficult to prevent the boys from disrupting the work. Therefore they chose to use a plain background and convey meaning through a combination of facial expressions, body language and text. We used a simple studio set-up for this – basic studio lighting and a plain backdrop. The girls felt the images should be in black and white because, as one of them put it, 'It gets the point across more clearly,' whereas 'colour is for happier photos'. While taking the photos they took turns in being behind and in front of the camera, those behind directing the action, encouraging those in front to enter into the spirit of the photo by imagining themselves in a real situation. In this way they managed to recreate the anger and frustration that they felt in order to make the final images more convincing. From the 26 images taken, five were chosen as being most successful.

Once these images had been printed the girls were encouraged to play with the text to see where it had most impact. They then

WE COULD BUILD

MORE THAN HOUSES

IF WE HAD THE CHANCE.

decided it should be short and to the point. I brought examples of other photographers' work into school for them to look at, and one girl was particularly interested in the work of Barbara Kruger, whose use of text she felt 'jumped out at you'. Having agreed on this style for their project, they wanted the images printed as large as possible. The result was a series of 12x16 inch posters that were displayed in the school library. I felt that the work was a clear example of the way in which the girls had developed an understanding of photography's potential to present clear and powerful messages.

In the Primary National Curriculum documents it states that children should have 'opportunities to *participate* and *initiate* on equal terms', and that the classroom environment should present 'opportunities for a variety of groupings'. The English document clearly supports work around media education, suggesting that the taking of photographs gives children a chance to 'express ideas and feelings and develop critical reflection'. Although within the recommendations there is no specific mention of single-sex groups, by working in the ways we did the above objectives were covered.

The documents also suggest that teachers work together, and that non-teaching assistants, parents and other adult helpers contribute the time to facilitate the provision of small-group work.

The majority of primary teachers' and helpers' posts are filled by women, and by working together to encourage and support groups of girls to explore and articulate their feelings they will not only be complementing schools' equal opportunities policies, but will gain a greater insight into how girls feel about the environment in which they work.

no more gadgets and trousers:
the practical bit

getting started

I t is useful to see photography as Emmet Gowin describes it, 'as a tool for dealing with things everybody knows about but isn't attending to'. Along these lines we suggest some simple starting points for work. Think of all the places you have lived. How many of these places have you photographed? Or the rooms in them? Then there's work. In how many places have you worked? What type of record do you have of that? The outing, the celebration dinner, or something more revealing involving another way of looking at it? There are all those meals eaten or cooked; all those people who faced each other across breakfast, dinner, supper, snacks, nightcaps, booze-ups. There are babies with bottles and babies at breasts. What about all the discussion and arguments that have gone on in your home? Did you dare to pick up a camera at the time, swap it back and forth with your tormentor and record what you were doing? Imagine the immense spectrum of images that could have been sliced, or frozen; all the scenarios of human interaction in which you have been involved. Now think of the limited range of images on offer in the general and photographic press. Perhaps use a press photograph as a starting point for a collage. Lay your own pictures around it to say something quite different.

What is important about photographs kept by families, together with school reports, infant hair and teeth, household documents, newspaper cuttings and letters, is that they constitute a rich source of information about a particular family at a particular time in history, occupying a particular social position. Most families keep only a few of what could be called 'building materials' towards an archive; most do not keep diaries, household books or 'visual lifelines'. It is usually just the pictures that are kept and these depend for meaning on the context in which they are produced, or reproduced, or used. The context of most family pictures is the family itself, yet it is in that very family, which is caught up in power struggles, or straitjacketed in 'universal' taboos – for example, incest or domestic violence – or personal taboos around what is considered to be respectable and shameful, that more is kept hidden than is revealed. In addition, family archives are in relationship to other types of institutional archive so that anything approaching a whole picture is impossible to come by. We are suggesting ways of ordering our celebrations, rituals, testimonials, fantasies and facts so that at least we understand that the family archive mediates knowledge and power in the family, as do archives in the public arena.

Within each of our families we negotiate minefields of what can and cannot be spoken about. The aim is to understand the dynamics within the relationships. Try to imagine what photographs you could take if you wanted to open up some really explosive discussions around the subject of, for instance, family Christmas. Take an imaginary roll of film next Christmas: take the snapshots in your head and write a text to go with it.

Visual lifelines
Begin by collecting any photographs you can lay your hands on. Borrow and xerox what people won't part with. Sort them out into chronological order. Next, lay them out in a long line right across the floor. If you have clusters of images taken at certain dates and very little at others, lay them out in clumps or single photographs. Do not worry about what is missing. When you have done this – and it might take you right down the hall and out of the front door – start to work out the actual years/dates you have travelled through, adding the dates under each block on a piece of paper. Choose a single image to represent each year or key event in your life. Throw into the original pile everything that does not seem significant. You will end up with a selection of photographs mapping out your life in a totally different way from that which has ever represented you before. Now begin to separate when the photographs were taken from the reasons why they were taken and try to remember who took them. This information constitutes the beginnings of your visual lifeline, or self-history, which you can build on and develop in your own particular way. For instance, take one or two photographs from your 'self-history' and find a quiet space to do some detailed work on them. This can take the form of talking into a tape-recorder or writing in a diary or scrapbook. Say everything you can think of about the photograph as a way of getting your memories moving, including those you might not want to remember. Make notes about pictures which might have been taken but never were, or things that you regret not being recorded.

A 'here and now' way of working could run concurrently with the history work. This could be a process of making new images and putting them in context. The simplest expansion of the family album idea is to think in terms of the journal or diary form. Mix, as a social scrapbook, the writing you do, the bits of public information relevant to what you are recording, your own and other images and so on. Adding photographs to a diary can transform it. Tristine Rainer's *The New Diary: How to Use a Journal for Self Guidance and Creativity* can be usefully adapted to the idea of making a photo-diary. This can be a way of speaking for and to yourself, of finding various ways of externalising interior monologue. The best way to start is in the present. Try to express something to yourself, with an image, a description of a feeling, a poem, a cutting from a newspaper or magazine.

Modern cameras are useful for diary work, as most of them have a built-in device which allows you to take a delayed-action picture. You set up and focus on something 'standing in' for yourself, set the camera, then move into frame to include yourself in the picture. Perhaps take your picture every morning for a week immediately you get out of bed or maybe visit a photo booth when you are able and stick the pictures into a book. Date everything. Such pictures will give little indication about your life, but they may be touchstones reminding you how you felt at given moments in your history. The slightest change of facial expression, if it is your own, can trigger off a flood of connotation and memories about yourself at certain periods. There is no need to keep your diary consistently. Just do what you feel is necessary and possible.

Documenting everyday living

As a solo project
Photographing everyday life can be as mundane, as exciting, or as thoughtful as you want to make it. There are so many ways of doing this. It might be pleasurable to go on a monthly walk at a regular time and photograph anything new which may have appeared since last you looked. So many things get torn down that sometimes it becomes impossible to remember what went before. Buildings come and go all the time, as well as the advertising hoardings that cover all the demolition and rebuilding. So many things are ephemeral. Accumulate 'evidence' of the world around you. Choose a theme – it could be news hoardings, or posters indicating the kind of entertainment going on or revealing the struggles going on in the area; changing housing, exteriors or new properties going up, or even the signs trying to sell them. Another productive way of working is to take eight or nine fortnightly walks, always taking the same route, in your immediate locality or high street. This is an open-ended way of proceeding, simply

photographing what you find interesting around you. Shift the time of day you take the walk. A building that looks sedate or deserted at one point springs to life at another. Engage with details, like how many shops have cats in the windows, or what advertisements are on the sides of buses. You can start off doing this inside your head rather than with a camera so that you learn to use your eyes differently. You begin to grasp how transient things are and how much of the world we miss when our minds are preoccupied.

The focal point of documenting everyday life could be a portrait. Make a close-up photographic portrait of someone in your family, or a friend or partner. Concentrate on making him or her look as good as possible. Then stage another shot to show the person at work or doing something active. Think about the differences between the pictures and what they do and do not show.

As a group project
One of the problems of working in groups arises when the only common interest in the group is in photography itself. Where does one begin with no shared set of values? The best way to get pleasure and information and to accommodate everybody is to suggest a project on photographic style.

A good starting point could be the local park. Within this confined space you could employ a 'documentary' technique (capturing slices of life as they occur): watching park workers, sports activities, loungers, children and those involved in the care of those children; or you could adopt a romantic, aesthetic approach, concentrating on the rural aspects of the same locality, taking panoramic scenes of the pond, under- or over-exposing them to create mood, or colour close-ups of the roses and trees.

Working in this way means that a joint miniature exhibition can be aimed at, to demonstrate not only what is going on in your local area, but also how the same subject matter is affected by different stylistic treatments. The number of styles people can get to grips with initially will be fairly limited, but there will be enough scope to broaden into a general discussion of how we get pleasure from different things and how two people standing side by side with their cameras will convey totally different information. This kind of group could run over a number of weeks and could include, if a darkroom is available, darkroom work with its many options.

Saying what we already know
Shooting a photo story can be an exciting group project. Photo stories have now become an apparently indispensable way of life for young women in their magazines. They are also integral to much crime and romantic fiction and of course to some types of comic. Because they use photographs they appear to be more 'real' than drawings. As a form of entertainment, of pleasure-giving, of

tension-raising, of happy never- or ever-after endings, they are without parallel.

Shooting a photo story takes time. Work it all out initially in a discussion group where you throw up possible themes, then carefully script your story. Work out locations, choose your actors and gather whatever props you need. Shoot it in one or two sessions, keeping as close as you can to your storyline but remaining open to serendipity. The real work takes place when the colour prints come back. You could argue for several sessions over what you wanted to say, or it could be settled in a few minutes. The shooting of a photo story is often a good way to understand what different lenses do (close-up, mid-shot, long-shot). Make sure that when a close-up is needed, this is done at the framing and shooting stages and not left to the darkroom stage. Making or using a photo story can be an immensely pleasurable form of radical photo practice. It is also a very enjoyable way to work with children.

FACE VALUES

Another group project: invite women who 'do not like their own faces' to come to a meeting to discuss this phenomenon. Each participant would bring an informal portrait, with room/window lighting, as a way of beginning to open up discussions. It is easier to talk about pictures than real faces. In the group we organised it transpired that each person wondered what on earth the others did not like about their faces, and what had brought them to the meeting. It seemed inconceivable that this lively, friendly, sarcastic, worldly bunch of women could have so many hang-ups. Nor did they see much connection between the photographs produced and the evidence of their own eyes. Lively discussion arose around the split between how people felt about themselves, what they had internalised as fear and what other people actually saw in their living, walking, dynamic interacting selves. It became more and more obvious that each of us had fixed images of our faces, the culmination of years of scrutiny in mirrors and indoctrination from the media, from friends and family. Each flaw had been logged according to some invisible and unconscious criterion. Each baggy eye, wrinkle, spot, double chin, crooked nose, broken hair end had been included in a personal inventory of shame unfolding a persecuting map of all our faults. Moreover, as we increased in age, these inventories expanded.

Such a group could be a useful way of dealing with anxiety in a supportive situation. Building on this there is potential for its reversal through 'public' display, fun and pleasure. People brought make-up, clothes, wigs, props – anything that could contribute to confronting old fears and creating new fantasies.

We broke up into pairs. Working without mirrors we trustingly offered up our faces to a partner who could do whatever kind of make-up she liked. After this initial stage, which was fearful and downright funny, people dressed up and photographed each other.

The activity moved then into writing. The dressing-up clothes and make-up were removed and people spent five minutes gazing at themselves in their mirrors. Now was the time to write what they were feeling. This could remain as private as they wished it to be. We came together as a group to end the meeting by talking about our experience of the workshop.

taking the pictures

When I was first asked to write the chapter on the technical side of taking photographs I balked at the idea. Surely enough has been written in popular photographic literature to cover all the information needed? On second thoughts, I began to realise that much is written in books and magazines on the assumption that the reader is mainly interested in gadgetry. Moreover, the illustrations, which include a liberal sprinkling of nude females and young women in 'glamour' settings, are of little interest to the reader of this book who wishes to express herself in a personal way and record her life and interests through her photographs. In these publications 'tricky effects' are encouraged and called 'creative' whereas true creativity lies in the original expression of an idea or concept, confidence arising through the use of foolproof equipment which leaves one free to concentrate on the subject. Skills can be left to accumulate with practice and experience as with any other activity and a serious review of what can be improved both technically and visually helps to speed the process.

Which camera?
This is as broad a question as asking 'What car do I need?' Your choice is dictated by how much you can afford (remembering basic accessories, film and processing) and what you really need. Consider the size and weight of the camera. I don't lug heavy equipment up an icy mountainside and have taken good photographs with a compact camera. Compact cameras are small and can be stashed in a pocket or bag ready for immediate use. Larger cameras are heavy and are more likely to need supporting with a tripod.

Whichever camera you buy, read the instructions until you understand them, as you would with any new piece of equipment. Run a trial film through the camera and test the various facilities, taking notes so that you will be able to analyse the results when the film is processed. Do not be daunted by the camera! If you are planning to take pictures of a wedding or on holiday, be familiar with the camera before you start. It is important to avoid panic. If you can learn to use a word processor, set up a video-recorder, drive a car or ride a bicycle, you can certainly learn to use a camera. Even if the first attempts are not perfect, it's not the end of the world. Try again and learn from your mistakes.

I recommend 35mm cameras as the ideal format to start with. Most 35mm films are easily purchased and prints from negatives, enlargements and transparencies for projection are processed everywhere.

I recommend *Which Camera?*, which you can buy at the local newsagent's, as being excellent reading before choosing a camera. Ask a friend who knows about cameras – but beware of the camera buff or you could buy more than you need! If you possibly can, borrow (or hire) a camera of the type you are interested in and try it out.

Second-hand cameras and accessories are advertised in the amateur photography magazines and in *British Journal of Photography*. Another source of supply for used equipment is through some photographic galleries, clubs and societies. Always try to check equipment if you buy it through a private source.

What is a camera?

A camera is a light-proof box with a lens through which reflected light from the subject travels to reach the light-sensitive film in the box. Focus controls sharpen the image. The focus distance is marked with symbols or, more commonly, feet or metres. The shutter controls the duration of time that the light falls on the film by opening and closing. The shutter speeds are usually measured in fractions of a second. The aperture (or f-stop) is a variable size and is usually an iris diaphragm in modern cameras. The control of the aperture size fixes the amount of light (brightness) that reaches the film and the depth of focus. It is measured in f-stops.

The most common camera types

There are other cameras on the market but I have noted the main types here. All major advantages are marked *.

SIMPLE VIEWFINDER CAMERA

Good for 'happy snaps' and all situations where a more expensive, sophisticated camera is at risk, such as on a beach, where sand and salt water might get into the works. Some viewfinder cameras are disposable and therefore good for children to learn on. Quick and instant to use.

*Inexpensive
Made of plastic and therefore easily damaged
*Lightweight
Not all take 35mm film
Some have limited film-speed settings
Most effective when used in good light
Simple to use but no choices as to exposure or focus
Not many have flash facility
No close-up focus

COMPACT CAMERAS

These are used by 60 per cent of the contributors to this book. Their compact design and lightness make them easy to carry around in all situations. They are ideal for most outdoor group and family portraits, landscapes and still life. Not all cameras will focus closer than 1.5 metres (4 feet 6 inches), which will limit the close-up work. Remember that if there are low light levels or if the subject is fast-moving and there is no flash facility it will be necessary to use a fast film. Check the film-speed settings on the camera. Not all conditions are suitable for using the flash as either the subject can be too far away or the flash will not cover the full subject area.

The more advanced compact cameras can be used for all the above and also for interiors, action shots and night photography. The override on the automatic facilities will enable you to experiment with focus, exposure and flash.

Cameras with variable focal-length lenses and zoom lenses will allow for changing the distance of the subject in the picture from the camera. Distant subjects can be brought nearer at the press of a button or, with portraits, the subject can fill the frame.

Check the focusing range of these compact cameras. Some will not focus closer than 1.5 metres. With the autofocus facility take care to override the focusing when you are taking photographs through glass or reflections in a mirror or it will focus on the glass surface, not on the reflected image. This is done by pointing the camera to a subject of equivalent distance to that of camera to glass added to the distance of the glass to reflected subject and using the focus lock by half depressing the shutter-release button. Point the camera towards the subject again without altering the button, and shoot.

Simple compact camera

Check possibility of variable film speeds

Fixed focus or *autofocus

*Choice of symbol f-numbers

Most have *auto-exposure

Autofocus compact camera

Check type of battery required. Some are expensive

*Manual focus or *autofocus

*Some have choice of focal-length settings

*Some have zoom lenses

*Fill-in flash facility, *some with red-eye elimination

*Some have flash override

SINGLE-LENS REFLEX CAMERAS

These cameras are the more versatile and sophisticated version of the compact cameras and the 35mm camera most used by professional photographers. They have a very accurate viewing and focusing facility. Many cameras will have accessories and a range of lenses.

Not all are automatic
*Most have interchangeable lenses
*Through-the-lens metering, some automatic
*Other equipment can be added (e.g., for close-up photography)
*Sophisticated flash system can be added to the camera

I am not dealing with medium- and large-format cameras. If you become interested in these, I recommend that you try them out by joining an evening class where there are studio facilities and a range of equipment and studio lights. Many evening institutes and adult education centres have courses in photography.

Lens types

All the lenses mentioned here refer to 35mm film and cameras.

The three basic lens types for the 35mm camera are the short focal-length lenses (wide-angle), from 21mm to 35mm; the standard or normal lenses, from 40mm to 55mm; and the long focal-length lenses (telephoto), from 80mm to 135mm. Added to these are the range of zoom lenses which have variable focal lengths ranging from 24–35mm, 35–105mm or 70–210mm. Most 35mm SLR camera bodies with the interchangeable lens facility are sold with a standard lens.

35mm compact cameras with built-in zoom lenses usually have a variable focal length from 35–80mm which covers wide-angle through to a 'portrait' telephoto. Other compact cameras come with wide-angle lenses with a fixed focal length, usually of 35mm.

There are many other lenses available with more specialised uses, such as the 55mm macro lens for close-up work, which can also be used as a standard lens; the longer focal-length lenses for natural history photography; fish-eye lenses and variable shift lenses for architectural work.

Standard lenses are the workhorse of the range and can be used for most purposes. Wide-angle lenses have a large depth of field and a wide angle of view which makes this type of lens ideal for photographing small rooms, landscapes and architecture. With limited space for manoeuvre this type of lens becomes indispensable. These lenses are difficult to use for portraits as features can appear distorted when the sitter is close to the camera. The more extreme wide-angle lenses should not be tilted from the exact vertical or you will get distortion.

Lenses: focal length makes a difference.

Photos: Joan Solomon

Long focal-length or telephoto lenses bring a distant subject nearer. As they have a narrow depth of field this can be exploited by having the background out of focus and thereby isolating the subject from the background. Lenses of focal length of around 80mm are ideal for portrait work as the photographer is not working on top of the sitter and can therefore develop a more relaxed relationship with the model. Great care has to be taken with long focal-length lenses not to get camera shake. The rough rule of thumb for hand-held cameras is not to use a shutter speed slower in fractions of a second than the focal length of the lens used. Therefore a lens with a focal length of 200mm needs to be used with a shutter speed of not slower than $1/250$ second and a 80mm lens with a shutter speed of not slower than $1/125$ second, which is the generally recommended slowest shutter speed for any hand-held cameras.

Basic camera accessories
Use a camera case. All equipment needs to be protected from knocks, weather and dust. It is most important to have a bag that you can get into easily. If you have to rummage for a new roll of film you could well lose the shot! Separate compartments in the gadget bag will protect lenses from dust and knocks.

I have a very tattered but serviceable padded gadget bag which doubles as a purse and passport-carrier when I'm travelling abroad. It doesn't look anything special, which can be an advantage in some less savoury areas.

It is most important to keep the equipment clean and free of dust and fingerprints, so lens tissues and puffer brush are important – and keep lens caps on the lenses when not in use.

Lens hoods cut out flare caused by extraneous light and thereby improve the quality of the photograph. I recommend using one if the camera allows, especially with wide-angle lenses. Some lenses have built-in lens hoods.

Filters
A filter is made of glass or plastic and is placed in front of the lens to modify the light reaching the film. Most filters cut down the amount of light reaching the film so you must give extra exposure. This increase is expressed in filter factors. Most compact cameras do not have filter threads on the lens but gelatin filters can be taped over the lens to give a reasonable result. Remember, with non-TTL metering you need to compensate for the reduced light reaching the film according to the filter factor.

Filters fall into three main categories: correction filters, polarising filters and 'effect' filters. I would also put in this category close-up attachments, although they are, strictly speaking, lenses.

When the camera design will allow, I recommend having a

Skylight 1B or UV filter permanently over each lens, not only to cut out blue cast of atmosphere or unwanted UV light, but also to protect the lens from dust, fingerprints (disastrous) and the weather. Filters are less expensive to replace than lenses.

filter	factor	f-stop	type of film	effect
UV	1	0	All film	Keeps the lens at all times as protector. Absorbs UV and penetrates haze
Skylight 1B	1	0	All film	Reduces blue cast in outdoor colour photography
NDx3	2	+1	All film	Neutral-density filters come in various densities. They reduce image brightness to: adjust film speed, decrease of depth of field, lower shutter speed
NDx4	4	+2		
NDx8	8	+3		
Graduated ND	Variable	Variable	All film	Use to equalise exposure of bright sky and darker ground
Polarising filter	3–4	$+1\,1/2–2$	All film	Cuts out most reflections. Darkens tone of sky when used at 90 degrees to sun
Yellow	2	+1	b/w	Slight darkening of sky tone
Orange	2.5	$+1\,1/3$	b/w	Darkens sky tone. Increases contrast between red and yellow. Good for sunsets
Red	8	+3	b/w	High contrast, sky dark, clouds white. Penetrates haze
Yellow/green	2.5	$+1\,1/2$	b/w	Balances skin tones. Good for landscape
Green	4	+2	b/w	Good for portraits in tungsten light
81A pale red	1.4	$+1/2$	Colour	Warms up flash or daylight on a dull day
80A	2.4	$+\,1\,1/3$	Daylight colour	Converts daylight film to tungsten film
80B	2	$+\,1$	Daylight colour	Converts daylight film to tungsten film. Use with photoflood lamps
85B	2.1	$+\,1$	Tungsten colour	Converts tungsten film to daylight film
CC30 magenta	2	$+\,1$	Colour	*Some* correction of colour balance in fluorescent light
CC40 magenta	2	$+\,1$	Colour	*Some* correction of colour balance in fluorescent light

Note that all coloured filters will affect the colour of the transparency or the colour print.

SLR cameras with through-the-lens metering will automatically adjust the change in exposure necessary for the filter used. 'Effect' filters range from soft focus, suitable for portraits, to starburst, multi-prism, graduated colour filters and so on. Coloured clear plastic, tights or clingfilm over the lens can also give interesting results and are cheap!

Camera support

A tripod camera support of some sort is essential for all photography using slow shutter speeds (less than 1/125 second). Tripods need to be heavy if used in a stiff wind for landscape photography and when the camera itself is heavy. Bean bags, a convenient wall or similar stable object are all useful as supports to keep the camera steady.

The film

There is a bewildering number of films to choose from. Get to know one film before trying another. Most films fall into two main categories: negative, from which positive prints are made, and positive film, which produces a direct positive image (transparency). Colour film can be either type; colour negative film can be conveniently processed and printed through the services of your local chemist. En prints are made and selected enlargements can be done to special order. This type of film is reasonably tolerant of exposure inaccuracies. Colour transparency (reversal) film requires accurate exposure. Not all colour reversal films will give the same result, even in identical conditions. Choose which you prefer – none is 'right'. Colour prints from this type of film are expensive but are not as difficult to print in a non-professional darkroom.

Black and white film is usually negative and is expensive to process and print unless you do it yourself. Chromogenic film (e.g., Ilford XP1) can be processed in colour negative chemicals and printed through the colour printing process. The result is usually sepia-toned but acceptable. Not all colour processing agents will take on this type of film, so ask first.

make	Agfa, Fuji, Ilford, Kodak, etc.
format	e.g., 35mm
film speed in ISO	The higher the number, the faster the speed
film type	Colour negative
	Colour transparency (reversal) – daylight or tungsten
	Black and white negative
	Black and white reversal and other specialist films
number of exposures	12, 24, 36
film processing date	Date by which film should be processed

The cheap films for sale from processing houses are made by the major manufacturers and packed with the processor's name and the quality is usually very good. Film details are clearly marked on the packet.

Check whether the film has DX barcode ratings which are necessary for most automatic compact cameras. Keep a record of the type and speed of film in the camera if you don't finish the film in one go. Store all film in the food compartment of a refrigerator in a waterproof box when not in use – both before and after exposure. Process films as soon as possible after exposing them.

Film speeds
Film comes in a range of speeds. Select according to the prevailing light conditions, the needs of the subject and the size of the final print.

film speed	lighting	best used for	picture quality
Slow 25–50 ISO	Bright daylight Studio lights/flash	Still subjects e.g., architecture, still life	Fine grain
Medium 64–200 ISO	Good daylight Studio lights/flash	All-purpose, family group, landscape	Medium grain
Fast 400 ISO	Dull daylight Mixed street lights	Exteriors, landscape sports photography, interiors with flash night shots with tripod Good to freeze movement	Grainy on enlargement
Very fast 1,000 ISO or more	Poor light	Use when flash not possible in poor light Good to freeze movement	Grainy on enlargement

Preparing to shoot
Always check the camera battery if you have not used the camera for some time. Carry spares.

1 Select film appropriate for subject.

2 Set film speed on the camera if it is not automatic.

3 Load camera and wind on to first exposure. Follow the instruction book carefully. Load in subdued light.

4 Calculate exposure and set f-number and shutter speed. (See 'Taking the exposure.') Not necessary if the camera is fully automatic.

5 Accurately frame the picture. Allow a small additional border all round for colour print film.

6 Focus. Some cameras have automatic focus. If the subject is not in the centre of the frame and you are using an automatic focus camera, point to the subject, lightly half depressing the shutter-release button. Then, keeping the button depressed, reframe the shot and shoot.

7 Take the photograph by pressing the shutter-release button gently.

8 Wind on for next exposure. (Not necessary if the camera has automatic wind-on.)

9 When the film is finished the camera will either automatically wind the film back into the cassette or you must rewind manually. Do not open the camera until you have completely rewound the film. The rewind handle will go slack when the action is completed.

Change of focus changes the reading.

Photos: Joan Solomon

Always stand in a steady position when taking photographs. Keep your elbows in and your feet slightly apart. Rest your elbows on a table or hold the camera against a wall for extra support. Hold your breath and gently squeeze the shutter-release button. Use a cable release and a tripod for avoiding camera shake on long exposures.

Focusing

Focusing the subject, even with autofocus cameras, must be done with care, particularly with close-up photography and when using long focal-length lenses. The technique to use for fast-moving objects (or if you do not wish to draw attention to yourself) is to pre-focus on a chosen spot and press the shutter when the subject reaches it. Autofocus cameras have to be 'tricked' into focusing on a subject reflected in or behind glass or when the centre of the picture area does not contain the subject. Point the camera to another subject the same distance from the camera and half depress the shutter-release button. Swing the camera back to the subject you wish to photograph and fully press down the button.

The selected aperture will affect the depth of field. It is not always necessary or even desirable to have the picture in sharp focus overall. Isolate your subject by having the background out of focus. Experiment and note how an out-of-focus subject against an in-focus ground can convey a different mood to the picture.

Taking the exposure

The exposure is the combination of shutter speed and aperture allowing the correct amount of light through the lens to reach the film. Some cameras will do this automatically – a useful facility for a beginner, but it eliminates any subtlety.

The simplest cameras have symbols to indicate the necessary f-number to use (sun, half-cloud with sun and cloud) combined with a non-variable shutter speed. It is recommended that a medium-speed film is used with this type of camera. Follow the recommended combinations of aperture and shutter speed given by the film manufacturer for various light conditions or use an exposure meter or the TTL meter in the camera. Here you will be given a range of different combinations of shutter speed and aperture (f-stop). All of these readings will allow the same amount of light to reach the film (the same exposure). Your choice will be dictated by the depth of field you need (the smaller the aperture the greater the depth of field), the shutter speed suitable for the subject (fast shutter speeds freeze movement), and whether you're hand-holding the camera or using a tripod (use a tripod or other support for slower than $1/125$-second exposures).

Metering through the camera/integrated reading
Point the camera to the subject and focus. Set the apertures desired and change the f-stops on the lens until the needle in the viewfinder points to the correct exposure. Conversely, set the aperture and change the shutter speed until the correct combination is indicated. If a landscape has a large area of sky, point the camera down to include more of the ground and take a reading. Return to the original view, reset the exposure to an average sky/ground reading, or the ground reading only. This will avoid under-exposure of the shot. When a subject is backlit, open up one stop. When a light subject is against a dark ground, move in and take a reading and then step back, reset the camera and expose.

Independent meter reading
I recommend a separate hand-held meter for any person who is aiming to take photography seriously. Not only is the meter a back-up to the camera meter reading, but it can measure reflected light from the subject as well as incident light (light falling on the subject) if an attachment is used. The film speed is set on the meter and a reading of the light level taken. The various possible combinations of shutter and f-stops are shown when the needle is set to the reading. Some subjects have to be compensated for. Snow scenes might need up to two stops more exposure than the meter will indicate. This phenomenon is due to the meter reading to an average 18 per cent grey which does not exist in overall lighter-than-average subjects. When in doubt always take several pictures and bracket the exposures. Take an average reading and expose one stop and half a stop over the meter reading exposure and then one stop and half a stop under. In this way you will learn which exposure is the most accurate in these light conditions and repeat it next time round. It helps to take a note of what you have done for later reference.

Judging the results

General faults

flare Picture taken directly into sun.
No lens hood used.

fogged film Usually due to loading/unloading the camera in bright light.

blurred picture	Camera shake, usually caused by pressing the shutter-release button too vigorously.
	Hand-holding the camera at too slow a shutter speed (below $1/125$ second).
	Use a tripod or a faster film if light is poor.
subject unintentionally blurred	Too slow a shutter speed to freeze movement.
dark unidentified blurs	Usually hair, fingers or camera strap in front of lens!
head cut off	Not enough care in framing. Allow for close-up with subjects 2 metres or less from camera when lens and viewfinder are separate on camera.
flash in night photograph too dark	Subject too far away for flash to cover.
	Flash obstructed.
red spots in eyes	Angle the camera away from full frontal flash or have subject looking away from flash to avoid red-eye.
reflections in glass/es, windows or mirrors	Tip spectacles slightly forward.
	Avoid using full frontal flash on all reflective surfaces.
	Shoot at 45 degrees from the shiny surface.
base fogging or colour distortion	Check that the film used was not out of date.

The quality of light/lighting the subject

Light, whether available or set up, should be used to create the illusion of solidity within the photograph. Light will also create the mood within the picture. Harsh, hard lighting looks very clinical and efficient whereas a soft desk lamp creates a feeling of intimacy and warmth.

The light source is considered in size in its relationship to the subject in the picture. The size of the light source will affect the quality of light and is best described as being large, medium or small. A ceiling used as a reflector (the light bounced off it) is a much larger light source than the sun in the sky or a lighted candle. A large light source, such as flash bounced off a ceiling or a floodlight with a large reflector, casts soft shadows and this gentle, if undramatic, light is ideal for photographing people and groups. The indirect light is easier for the sitter and the soft shadows well describe form. Medium light sources are more directional and cast more defined soft-edged shadows. A photograph taken near a window (interior) but away from direct sunlight or floodlight will give this type of lighting. Small light sources such as direct sun or flash or a studio spotlight on the subject give hard-edged shadows and small highlights and are less effective in creating the illusion of solid form. The contrast between highlight and shadow is often too great for use with colour film without secondary lighting to reduce the shadows (contrast).

The angle of the light to the subject is most important in the photograph. Full frontal lighting flattens out the subject whereas back lighting on its own shows the subject in silhouette. The effect

left Lighting: Anglepoise light above coffee pot. The last of the daylight. Result: Objects nearer the camera are in silhouette i.e., not enough detail. Note angle of shadows.

right Lighting: Hand-held lamp held slightly to right above camera. Result: Most objects are well defined and show surface detail and texture. Shadows are unobtrusive. The overall effect is 'natural' i.e., appears true to life.

of top lighting varies according to the size of the light source. A small light source looks hard and theatrical whereas a medium light source from a window or bounced from a reflector is excellent for a still life or portrait. Light from below, if it is the only source, can look ghoulish in a portrait. Side lighting is most frequently used in photography as it shows up detail and texture and gives a nice contrast with shadow. Half side lighting, the most frequently used, with more light towards the front, best describes the subject. The height of the light in relationship to the subject also changes the overall effect of side lighting. The subject can be separated from the background by using black card or a curtain in the window to cut off unwanted light.

It is rare to take a photograph without the need for a secondary light or 'fill-in' for the shadows. The secondary light in studio photography should not be as strong as the primary light and 'crossed shadows' caused by placing the secondary light directly into the shadow area should be avoided at all costs. It is simplest to use a reflector near the camera on the same side of the subject as the primary light source. Out of doors this is not so simple, although a white sheet or newspaper can make an effective reflector for small subjects and portraits – otherwise wait for a passing cloud!

Lighting a still life
The above illustrations show the set-up in my bedroom. The two lights used are my bedside lamp, which I could hand-hold at any angle and distance whilst still operating the camera, and an anglepoise. The fading daylight had little effect on the objects in the set-up but shows as a lighter tone in the background. The camera was held firm on a tripod. The lamps used were not adjusted for use with colour film.

The second photograph is not the definitive solution; just a possible one. Use light to show detail and texture, to describe the form (shape) of objects and to set the mood. Note that black and white film interprets colours into tones. A strong red, such as that of the coffee pot in the illustration, appears as a mid-grey. Because of this, the emphasis and balance of the set-up when translated into black and white can be very different from what is seen with the eye.

Flash as a light source
Most compact cameras have built-in flash. This can be used as the main light source, although the results are hard, or as a fill-in in daylight if the subject is in shadow. It is important to keep within the flash range to avoid 'fall-off' as it loses strength over short distances. If you choose to photograph a group of friends, have them grouped at the same distance from the camera rather than at different distances to avoid the figures further away being under-exposed. If they are closer than 1 metre they will appear too pale (over-exposed). Most medium-speed films will cope with the flash on subjects from about 1 to 3 metres. Compact cameras with built-in flash will vary, so follow the instructions and note the speed of the film you have in the camera. Batteries get used up fast if you use a lot of flash so make sure that the ready light shows before you take the shot.

Photographing moving subjects
The first thing is to decide whether you want to freeze movement, to 'catch' the moving object with a blurred background, or to have the moving object blurred against a sharp background. The first option will need a very fast shutter speed depending on how fast the subject is moving and its angle to the camera. Subjects moving across the picture plane (parallel to the camera) need faster shutter speeds than those moving at an angle to the camera. Do remember that sometimes it is more important to give the impression of the speed of the subject. A frozen-movement shot of a car looks as if it is parked! Panning with the moving subject will give a blurred background and gives the best feeling of it moving fast. Keeping the camera steady and using a slow shutter speed will result in the subject being blurred against a static ground. Shutter speeds will vary according to the speed of the moving object and the amount of 'blur' you want.

Composition
Framing or composing the picture is what many photographers find daunting. Firstly there is the option of using the camera vertically (portrait format) or horizontally (landscape format). Just because these formats are so named, there is no reason why landscapes should not be vertical or portraits horizontal. What is important is to compose the picture so that there is a good balance of design (structure), tone and/or colour, scale, texture, depth and space.
    Many photographers make the mistake of always taking

Lighting the same faces in a different way creates a very different image and meaning. Experimenting with this is very useful for 'identity' work.
Photos: Jo Spence

Reading photographs

The same picture can be 'read' in different ways. These photographs tell different stories to different people. When one image is juxtaposed with another it can be interpreted in yet another way.

above **Sue arriving. She is wearing a cycling helmet. Is she delivering a message or papers to Janet?**

centre **Sue showing a print to Janet. Both are now wearing aprons. What is Sue's work? Is she teaching? Learning? Consulting? What is Janet's role?**

below **Sue at an exhibition.**

Viewing the photographs together builds a more complete and accurate picture. In the individual pictures we read stereotypes. It is assumed that the woman wearing the helmet is delivering a paper or message to the woman in glasses. In fact Sue has just arrived at the studio. In the second picture, Sue is discussing colour with a fellow printer in the workshop. Janet, wearing the reading glasses, is not in charge. In the third, Sue is photographed at her exhibition of prints and paintings.

The photographs were taken with a telezoom compact camera on HP5 and processed and printed via the local chemist.

Framing pictures in different ways can change their meaning.

Photos: Joan Solomon

photographs at their own eye-level. Take a variety of pictures of the same subject; long shots and close-up, low eye-level and high viewpoints and compare them to see which best describe the situation. Putting them together as a mini collage creates new meaning. Pointing the camera upwards will cut out unwanted background detail. Moving close to the subject whenever possible will cut out details which are irrelevant to the picture. Broad landscape pictures are improved by linking the foreground to the sky (background) with an available tree, plant or figure. Sometimes framing the subject within another frame – literally a mirror or door – is effective both for portrait interiors and exterior photographs. A road or shadow or scattered objects leading into the picture will give a sense of depth. A light-toned figure set against a dark or textured background or a figure silhouetted against a light ground will stand out clearly and separately. Warm colours such as red and yellow show up very brightly in colour photographs. A 'touch' of red can enliven a picture with mainly dark colours but can be distracting when scattered overall if the main interest lies elsewhere. It must be remembered that strong colours in shade will not necessarily appear as bright as you wish in the print. Look at your photographs and see if you could improve them. Always aim to use the whole picture but see if you can improve the composition by using two L-shaped pieces of card to mask off or reframe the picture.

At the end of the day, it is not the beautifully composed picture that is most important – it is what you are saying with the photograph.

Glossary

Angle of view
Picture area covered when viewed through the lens.

Aperture
Variable size of opening through which a controlled amount of light travels through the lens to reach the film – calibrated in f-stops. The higher the f-stop number the smaller the aperture. Used in conjunction with shutter speed to control the exposure.

Aperture priority
System whereby the lens is manually preset and the shutter speeds are automatically adjusted to suit the light to give correct exposure.

ASA
American Standards Association. See ISO.

Autofocus
A system which automatically measures the distance from camera to subject and focuses the lens.

Bracketing
The additional exposure of the film, usually made in half- and one-stop increments both above and below the meter reading, to produce exact exposure.

'B' Setting
Bulb setting. The shutter remains open during the time that the shutter-release button is depressed. Use for long exposures.

Cassette
Light-tight container for 35mm film.

Compact camera
A small-format camera usually with automatic film and exposure setting, autofocus, film wind-on and rewind. Most have 35mm fixed focal-length lenses.

Computerised flash
Flash with a built-in photocell designed, when pre-set to the film speed and desired aperture, to automatically give the correct amount of light (exposure) up to a certain distance.

Contrast
Range of tones from highlights to darkest shadows affected by exposure, development and printing.

Cropping
Cutting off unwanted parts of the picture to improve the composition.

Depth of field
Distance between nearest and furthest point from the camera in which the subject will be in sharp focus.

DIN
Deutsche Industrie Norm. See ISO.

DX
Black and silver rectangles on cassette coded to automatically set the camera to the correct film speed and film length. This only functions in cameras with a compatible facility and must be set manually with all other equipment.

Enlargement
A print made larger than the negative or a print bigger than an en print.

En print
Machine-made print made from a 35mm negative usually 3.5x4.5 inches or 4x6.

Exposure
An exposure is made when the photosensitive material, usually film or paper, is exposed to a controlled amount of light for a controlled length of time.

Incident light reading
Measurement of light falling on the subject. To measure this hold the meter with a diffusing cell close to the subject pointing to the camera.

Reflected light reading
Measurement of light that is reflected from the subject to the camera. To measure this hold the meter close to the lens pointing to the subject.

Over-exposure
The exposure of photographic material to too much light resulting in dense negatives, dark positives or pale transparencies.

Under-exposure
Film or paper given insufficient light for the correct exposure. This results in too light-toned images and dark transparencies.

Fill-in
Light, either direct or reflected, used to lighten shadows.

Film

Colour reversal film
Positive film for colour transparencies which are projected for viewing.

Colour negative film
Negative film from which positive colour prints can be made.

Daylight film
Film designed to be used in daylight or with electronic flash.

Film speed
The measure of the sensitivity of the film to light. See ISO.

Reversal film
A film, usually a colour transparency, which is processed to make a positive.

Tungsten film
Colour transparency film for use in tungsten light.

Tungsten light
Light from household or photographic light bulbs.

Filters

Filter
Glass or gelatin placed in front of the lens to absorb specific wavelengths from the light passing through it or to reduce the amount of light passing through it to the film.

UV filter
Cuts down ultra-violet light which would otherwise affect colour film giving a blue cast.

Neutral density (ND) filter
Filters of different densities used

to reduce a measured amount of light reaching the film. Useful in very bright light conditions and when a slow shutter speed or wide lens aperture (narrow depth of field) is required.

Polarising filter
Filter (often rotated) to cut out reflections from non-metallic subjects and darken skies. Use between 45 and 90 degrees from angle of incidence of the light.

Flare
Direct light shining on the lens. Avoid this by using a lens hood and 'hide' the sun behind a convenient tree when shooting directly into the sun.

f-numbers
See Aperture.

Focus
The act of changing the lens to subject distance until a sharp image is formed.

Focus lock
Device to hold point of focus when moving on to another view – usually by half depressing the shutter-release button on a compact camera.

Format
The dimension of standard film and print size. A 35mm camera is a small-format camera.

Graininess
Visible grain showing on enlargement. Fast film is more grainy than slow film. Grain can be enlarged by deliberate action when processing black and white film.

Highlight
The brightest areas in the picture.

Infinity
Indicated as ∞. The distance 1,000 times or more than the focal length of the lens. The furthest point at which the camera will focus.

ISO
International Standards Organisation index for film speed rating replacing DIN and ASA.

Light
Artificial light
Any light other than daylight, including flash.

Available light
Any light by which the photograph can be taken without adding flash or further lighting.

Back light
Light coming towards the camera from behind the subject.

Backlit
A subject which is lit by back light; a *contre jour* photograph. Expose for the subject (shadow) to avoid under-exposing or use a fill-in flash.

Diffused light
Soft, shadowless lighting.

Flash
Bright light source of brief duration designed to fire at the instant the shutter is fully opened.

Lens
A device for bending light to a point of focus.

Lens hood
Device to shade the lens from unwanted light. Some lenses have built-in lens hoods. The hood should be compatible with the lens of the focal length for which it is designed.

Macro lens
Close-up lens for taking photographs at close range. Can also be used as a standard lens.

Normal lens
A normal (standard) lens on a 35mm camera has a focal length of 50mm, being approximately equivalent to the diagonal of the picture format (36mmx24mm).

Standard lens
See Normal lens.

Telephoto or long-focus lens
Lens with focal length greater than the diagonal of the image format, giving enlarged views of distant objects.

Wide-angle or short-focus lens
Lens with focal length less than the diagonal of the image format, giving a wide angle of view.

Zoom lens
Lens with variable focal length.

Panning
The act of swinging the camera, usually to follow a moving subject.

Photo montage
A selection of images arranged to make a single picture either by making a paste-up (collage) or by printing in the darkroom.

Positive
A print or transparency where the black and white tones or colours approximate those of the original view/subject.

Reflector
Any vehicle (white paper, foil, etc.) used to reflect light on the subject – usually to lighten shadows.

Self-timer
Mechanism on camera to delay the firing of the shutter by approximately ten seconds.

Shutter
A mechanism, fired by the shutter-release button, to control the time light remains on the film. Used in conjunction with aperture to control the exposure.

Shutter speed
The selected fraction of time the shutter is open to expose the film.

Single lens reflex (SLR)
A single-lens camera with a viewfinder system using a mirror and focusing screen.

Slide
A mounted transparency film ready for projection.

Transparency
See Slide.

TTL
Through the lens.

Viewfinder
Viewing part of camera for framing the picture. Usually shows focusing and exposure information (aperture and shutter speed set) on SLR cameras.

Sue Isherwood **recommended reading**

General

Heilbrun, Carolyn G., *Writing a Woman's Life*, The Women's Press, 1989.

Lynch, Dorothy and Richards, Eugene, *Exploding into Life: An Account with Photographs of an Encounter with Cancer*, Aperture in association with Many Voice Press, 1987.
Milner, Marion (aka Joanna field), *A Life of One's Own*, Virago, 1986.

Payne, Karen (ed), *Between Ourselves, Letters between Mothers and Daughters*, Picador, 1984.

Sligh, Clarissa, 'Reliving My Mother's Struggle' in *Liberating Memory: Our Work and Our Working-Class Consciousness*, Janet Zandy (ed), Rutgers University Press, 1994.

Warnock, Mary, *Memory*, Faber and Faber, 1987.

Educational

Dewdney, Andrew, Grey, Claire and Minnion, Andy, *Down But Not Out*, Trentham Books, 1994.

Dewdney, Andrew and Lister, Martin, *Youth Culture and Photography*, Macmillan Education/Arts Council, 1988. An introduction to photographic work with young people. The photo-text format explores the social and cultural expression of young people and is the result of six years' work with 14–16-year-olds in inner London.

Jayham, Jasmine and Walton, Kamina, *As Easy as ABC: A Teacher's Practical Guide*, Blackfriars Photography Project, 1989. An introduction to photography and language work in the primary classroom. Available from the The Photographer's Gallery Bookshop, London.

Family album, journals and diaries

Significant individual published diaries include those by:
Marie Bashkirtseff, Vera Brittain, Fanny Burney, Hannah Cullwick, Charlotte Forten Grimke, Fanny Kemble, Anaïs Nin, Sylvia Plath, Georges Sand, May Sarton, Mary Shelley, Sojourner Truth, Beatrice Webb, Virginia Woolf.

Davis, Thomas L., *Shoots: A Guide to Your Family's Photographic Heritage*, Travelling Light, 1978.

Ewald, Wendy, *Portraits and Dreams: Photography and Stories by Children of the Appalachians*, Writer and Readers, 1985.
Magic Eye: Scenes from an Andean Girlhood, Bay Press, 1992.

Hirsch, Julia, *Family Photographs: content, meaning and effect*, Oxford University Press, 1981.

Isherwood, Sue, *The Family Album*, Broadcasting Support Services, 1988. Available from Channel 4, Broadcasting Support Services, PO Box 4000, London W3 6XJ.

King, Graham, *Say 'Cheese'*, Collins, 1936.

Lifshin, Lyn, *Ariadne's Thread, A Collection of Contemporary Women's Journals*, Harper Colophon, New York, 1982.

Lesy, Michael, *Time Frames: the meaning of family pictures*, Pantheon Books, 1980.

Mann, Sally, *Immediate Family*, Phaidon, 1992.

Mass Observation Diaries, an Introduction, 1991, published jointly by Mass Observation (University of Sussex Library and the Centre for Continuing Education).

Miller, Alice, *Photography and images of childhood and fantasy pictures of a childhood*, Straus and Giroux, 1986.

Milner, Marion, *Eternity's Sunrise, A Way of Keeping a Diary*, Virago, 1987.

Rainer, Tristine, *The New Journal*, Angus and Robertson, 1980.

Stanley, Liz, *The Auto/biographical I, Theory and Practice in Feminist Auto/biography*, Manchester University Press, 1992.

What is a Family? Photographs and Activities about Families in Britain. Photography pack, Birmingham, December 1985. Available from Birmingham Development Education Centre, Gillett Centre, Selly Oak Colleges, Bristol Road, Birmingham B29 6LE.

Williams, Val, *Who's looking at the family?*, Barbican Art Gallery, 1994.

Gender and Sexuality

Betterton, Rosemary, (ed), *Looking On, Images of Femininity in the Visual Arts and Media*, Pandora, 1987.

Coward, Rosalind, *Female Desire*, Paladin, 1984. This deals with images of women and representation.

Meachim, Sally, Richards, Dave and Williams, Olukomi, *Focus for Change: Class, Gender and Race Inequality and the Media in an International Context*. Available from Reading International Support Centre, 103 London Street, Reading, RG1 4DA.

History

Coe, Brian and Gates, Paul, *The Snapshot Photograph, The Rise of Popular Photography 1888–1939*, Ash and Grant, 1977.

Hiley, Michael, *Victorian Women: Portraits from Life*, Gordon Fraser, 1989.

Williams, Val, *Women Photographers (The Other Observers 1900 to the Present Day)*, Virago, 1986.

Photography and photographic theory

Barthes, Roland, *Mythologies*, Vintage, 1993.
   Camera Lucida: Reflections on Photography, Vintage, 1993.

Berger, John, *Ways of Seeing*, Penguin, 1972. Based on a television series which explored the way in which photography took over traditions from painting in both representing property and women and the ways advertisements construct a world. *About Looking*, Writers and Readers, 1980.

Bezencenet, Steve and Corrigan, Philip, *Photographic Practices: Towards a Different Image*, Comedia, 1986.

Braden, Su, *Committing Photography*, Pluto Press/Arts Council, 1983.

British Journal of Photography, Timothy Benn Publishing Co.

Dick, Eddie and Moffat, Susan, *Picturing Women: Scottish Women in Photography*, Scottish Film Council/Hodder and Stoughton, 1991.

Evans, Harold (ed), *Pictures on a Page: Photo-journalism, Graphics and Pictures*, Heinemann, 1978. Explores the techniques of photography and photojournalism.

Hevey, David, *The Creatures Time Forgot, Photography and Disability Imagery*, Routledge, 1992.

Freund, Giselle, *Photography and Society*, Gordon Fraser, 1980.

Greenhill, Richard, Murray, Maggie and Spence, Jo, *Photography Guidelines*, Macdonald 1978.

Hall, Stuart, *Pictures of Everyday Life*, Comedia, 1986.

Holland, Patricia, Spence, Jo and Watney, Simon, (eds), *Photography Politics 2*, Comedia, 1987.

Isherwood, Sue and Stanley, Nick, *Creating Vision*, Cornerhouse Publications, 1994. An accessible introduction to ways of thinking about and making photographs.

Langford, Michael, *Starting Photography*, Focal Press, 1976. *Better Photography*, Focal Press, 1978. *Langford's 35mm Handbook*, Ebury Press, 1991.

Meigan, Paul and McWilliams, Bernard, *Photography Exposed*, Impact Books, 1984.

New Internationalist, 'Can I Take Your Picture? The Strange World of Photography', July issue, 1988. How photographs offer a highly selective view of the world. Highly recommended.

Partridge, Joe, *One Touch Photography*, Pan books, 1984.

Placca, Jane, Murray, Maggie and Prince, Brenda, *Desperately Seeking Pictures*, Arts Council, 1994. Women's photo-agency work.

Sekula, Allan, *Photography Against the Grain, Essays and Photo Works, 1973–83*, The Press of Nova Scotia College of Art and Design, 1984.

Ritchin, Fred, *In Our Own Image: The Coming Revolution in Photography*, Aperture, 1990.

Sligh, Clarissa, 'The Plaintiff Speaks' in *Picturing Us*, Deborah Willis (ed), The New Press, 1994.

Sontag, Susan, *On Photography*, Penguin. A series of general reflections on the development of photography.

Spence, Jo and Dennett, Terry, (eds), *Photography Politics 1*, Photography Workshop, 1979.

Spence, Jo, *Putting Myself in the Picture*, Camden, 1987.

Spence, Jo and Holland, Patricia, *Family Snaps: The Meanings of Domestic Photography*, Virago, 1991.

Tagg, John, *The Burden of Representation: Essays on Photographics and Histories*, Macmillan, 1988.

Which Camera? Bi-monthly, Evro Publishing Co. Ltd, 60 Waldegrave Road, Teddington, Middlesex, TW11 8LG.

Therapy-related books

Akeret, Dr Robert U., *Photoanalysis: How to interpret the hidden psychological meaning of personal photographs*, Fireside Books, Simon and Schuster, 1973.

Dickson, Anne, *A Woman in Your Own Right, Assertiveness and You*, Quartet Books, 1982.

Ernst, Sheila and Maguire, Marie, *Living with the Sphinx: Papers from the Women's Therapy Centre*, The Women's Press, 1987.

Glouberman, Dina, *Life Choices and Life Changes Through Imagework (The art of developing personal vision)*, Unwin Paperbacks, 1989.

Krzowski, Sue and Land, Pat, (eds), *In Our Experience: Workshops at the Women's Therapy Centre*, The Women's Press, 1988.

Miller, Alice, *Thou Shalt Not Be Aware: Society's Betrayal of the Child*, Pluto Press, 1985.
The Drama of Being a Child, Virago Press, 1987.
The Untouched Key: Tracing Childhood Trauma in Creativity and Destructiveness, Virago, 1990.

Orbach, Susie and Eichenbaum, Louise, *Bitter Sweet: Love, Envy and Competition in Women's Friendships*, Arrow books, 1987.

Quilliam, Susan and Grove-Stephenson, Ian, *The Counselling Handbook*, Thorsons, 1990. A complete guide to what to expect and how to get the counselling you need.

Silverstone, Leisl, *Art Therapy, The Person Centred Way*, Autonomy Books, 1993.

Skynner, Robin and Cleese John, *Families and How to Survive Them*, Methuen, 1983.

Steedman, Carolyn, *Landscape for a Good Woman: a story of two lives*, Virago, 1986. A psychoanalytic account of a working-class life.

Weiser, Judy, *Phototherapy Techniques*, Jossey Bass, 1993.
Exploring the secrets of personal snapshots and family albums.

Photography and media centres and workshops

Ashbourne
The Photographers' Place,
Bradbourne, Ashbourne,
Derbyshire DE6 1PB
Tel: 01335 25392

Bath
F Stop Gallery and
Darkrooms
Green Park Station
Bath BA1 1JB
Tel: 01225 316922

Batley
Artimedia
21 Batley Field Hill
Huddersfield WF17 OBQ
Tel: 01924 442598

Birmingham
Building Sights
Custard Factory No.1
Gibb Street,
Digbeth, Birmingham 9
Tel: 0121 608 7006

Wide Angle
c/o Centre for Media Arts
7 Frederick Street,
Birmingham B1 3HE
Tel: 0121 233 4061

Bradford
National Museum of
Photography
Pictureville, Prince's View,
Bradford BD5 0TR
Tel: 01274 727488

Bristol
Watershed Media Centre
1 Canons Road,
Bristol BS1 5TX
0117 9276444

Broomfield
Photographers at Duckspool
Duckspool Farm,
Broomfield,
Quantock Hills,
Somerset TA5 2EG
Tel: 01823 451305

Cambridge
Cambridge Darkroom
Dales Brewery
Gwydir Street
Cambridge CB1 2IJ
Tel: 01223 350725

Cardiff
Media Education Wales
Cardiff Institute of Higher
Education
Cyncoed Centre
Cyncoed Road
Cardiff CF2 6XD
Tel: 01222 689101/2

Colchester
Signals
Essex Media Centre
21 St Peter Street
Colchester C01 1EW
Tel: 01206 560255

Derby
Metro Cinema Gallery
Green Lane
Derby DE1 1SA
Tel: 01332 40170

Edinburgh
Portfolio Gallery
43 Candlemaker Row
Edinburgh EH1 2QB
Tel: 0131 220 1911

Exeter
Exeter Darkroom
Exeter & Devon Arts Centre
Gandy Street
Exeter EX4 3LS
Tel: 01392 432617

Glasgow
Street Level
279–281 High Street
Glasgow G4 OQS
Tel: 0141 552 2151

Leeds
Pavilion Women's
Photography Centre
2 Woodhouse Square
Leeds LS3 1AD
Tel: 0113 2431749

Vera Productions
30–38 Dock Street
Leeds LS10 1JF
Tel: 0113 2428646

Leicester
Picture House Gallery &
Media Education Centre
113 Princess Road East
Leicester LE1 7LA
Tel: 0116 2549083

Liverpool
Open Eye Photography
110–112 Bold Street
Liverpool L1 6EN
Tel: 0151 708 5699

Young Women's Media
Project
The Royal Institution
Colquilt Street
Liverpool L1 4DE
Tel: 0151 709 9419

London

The ARTEC Project
393–395 City Road
London EC1
Tel: 0171 833 1875

The Art of Change
Level 3
Lion Court
435 The Highway
Wapping
London E1 9HT
Tel: 0171 702 8802

Camerawork
121 Roman Road
Bethnal Green
London E2 0QN
Tel: 0181 980 6256

Monochrome Women's
Photography Collective
Clapham Pool
141 Clapham Manor Street
London SW4 6DB
Tel: 0171 926 0703

Photofusion
17a Electric Lane
Brixton
London SW9 8LA
Tel: 0171 738 5774

Women's Artists' Slide
Library
Media Education Centre
Fulham Palace
Bishops Avenue
London SW6 6EA
Tel: 0181 731 7618

Manchester

Counter Image
3rd Floor, Faser House
36 Charlotte Street
Manchester M1 4FO
Tel: 0161 228 3551

Workers Film Association
Media & Cultural Centre
9 Lucy Street
Manchester M15 4BX
Tel: 0161 848 9782

Middlesbrough

Cleveland Arts
7–9 Eastbourne Road
Linthorpe
Middlesbrough TS5 6QS
Tel: 01642 812288

Oxford

Oxford Photography
Department of Visual Arts
Oxford Brookes University
Gipsy Lane
Headington
Oxford OX3 0BP
Tel: 01865 483477

Sheffield

Untitled Gallery
1 Brown Street
Sheffield S1 2BS
Tel: 0115 2725947

Southampton

Mount Pleasant Photography
Workshop
Mount Pleasant Middle
School
Mount Pleasant Road
Southampton
Tel: 01703 231977

West Bromwich

Jubilee Arts
84 High Street
West Bromwich
West Midlands B70 8HP
Tel: 0121 553 6862

about the contributors

Nilofar Akmut is originally from Pakistan. A sculptor trained at the Slade School of Art, she has for many years lived between two cultures. She now lives and works in the UK and exhibits in Britain, Europe and Japan.

Sylvia Ayling trained to become a teacher as a mature student and now works as a part-time English teacher in women's groups.

Lisa Chell was brought up on a farm. She studied art in Leicester and now works as a sculptor.

Claire Collison initially studied English and drama at Goldsmith's. She is currently images editor for *Disability Arts* magazine. She exhibits at a number of galleries around the country and has been published in *Camerawork* and *Available Light*.

Alice Dennett is a pensioner and shares a roof with her husband in Eastbourne in Sussex. They have two grown-up children and six grandchildren.

Janet Edmeades is an artist who uses photography in evolving autobiographical work. Her background is in theatre design and sculpture. She works in arts and disability organisations in Bristol.

Beryl Graham was involved in teaching photography before becoming head of photography at Projects UK, a media arts centre in Newcastle. She is now a freelance curator and writer with a special interest in photography and new technology, based in San Francisco and Newcastle. She is currently researching interactive computer-based art for an MPhil/PhD at the University of Sunderland.

Claire Grey teaches photography in schools and community education and was one of the workers involved in a project which led to the 'Down But Not Out' exhibition held at King's Cross station (London) in 1988.

Anne Hickmott is a lecturer in photography and an artist working in the media of photography, holography and print-making. She has exhibited in the US, Canada, the UK and Germany. She lives and works in London.

Sue Isherwood is an arts administrator and educator and an Open University tutor on women's studies courses. She lives in Somerset.

Joyce Leketi-Solomon is a black South African 24-year-old who was adopted into a white family as a baby and has grown up in the UK. She has now completed her BA in humanities and lives and works in Bristol.

Rosy Martin works as a designer, lecturer, workshop leader and phototherapist. She lives and works in London.

Maggie Murray is a freelance photographer and founder member of Format Photographers, the women's photo agency. Her work has appeared in books, magazines and exhibitions and she speaks regularly at conferences and workshops.

Brenda Prince is a freelance photographer and a partner/member of Format Photographers, the women's photo agency. She studied photography at the Polytechnic of Central London. She has exhibited at a number of galleries around the country and her work has appeared in a variety of publications and books. She remains firmly committed to the idea of taking 'positive' images of women, gay people, and other under- or misrepresented people in society.

Clarissa Sligh comes from a southern African-American working-class background and has worked as a computer programmer in NASA, a financial analyst on Wall Street and a university and college teacher. Her work is based on creating personal and community narratives in mixed-media installations and she has exhibited in a variety of galleries including the Walker Art Centre in Minneapolis, MOMA and the Schomburg Centre for Research in Black Culture in New York, and the Australian National Gallery in Canberra.

Joan Solomon is an educationalist, photographer and writer who trained as a photo theoretician. She is a pioneer of photographically illustrated multi-cultural books for children in Britain and works throughout the country under the aegis of the Writers in Schools Scheme. Joan has designed and run joint workshops with Jo Spence on 'Autobiography/Contexting the Self through Photography and Writing' and has been resident tutor at the Watershed in Bristol. She lives in Bristol.

Jo Spence was a writer and artist of international repute. Her work has been exhibited in Europe, North America, Australia, Japan and England. She was co-founder, with Terry Dennett, of Camerawork and Photography Workshop. She did much to politicise debates in and around independent photography through an interface of the psychic, the social and the ideological. Jo died in 1992.

Jo Stanley is a freelance writer and cultural worker and is particularly involved in exploring older women's history. Her most recent book is *Bold in her Breeches: Women Pirates Across the Ages* (Pandora, 1995). She also edited the late Jo Spence's collected works, *Cultural Sniping: the Art of Transgression* (Routledge, 1995). Originally from a Liverpool working-class family, her home is now in north London, where she is struggling to live generously and radically despite the social climate.

Linda Troeller is an artist who lives and works in New Jersey, USA. Her photographs have appeared in numerous magazines and the *TB/AIDS Diary* has been exhibited in galleries, hospitals and schools in the USA, Europe and Mexico.

Kamina Walton began developing the use of photography in primary education in 1987. Since that time she has worked for a wide variety of organisations, has co-written a booklet, *As Easy as ABC*, on photography and language work in the primary classroom. She now lives and works as a freelance photographer in Bristol and has recently been researching and writing a book for the Arts Council of England, *Picture My World: Photography in Primary Education*.

Elizabeth-Anne Williams lives in Staffordshire, has an MA in photographic studies and now runs a photographic gallery in the Midlands.

Jean Wythe is a pensioner and a writer and member of the Federation of Writers and Poets.